ATM

40 YEARS
OF BUSES IN
MANCHESTER

BY

JOHN A SENIOR MCIT

Venture *publications*

CONTENTS

ISBN 1 898432 65 1 © JA SENIOR SEPTEMBER 1995
COMPUTERISED PRODUCTION FOR THE PUBLISHERS BY
MOPOK GRAPHICS 128 PIKES LANE, GLOSSOP, DERBYSHIRE

FOREWORD

Forty years ago when I started taking colour photographs of buses and trolleybuses in and around Manchester I was fascinated by the number of operators to be seen, if you knew where to look and when. Twenty years ago I had lost interest; everywhere the same spick and span orange and white buses – oh for the variety of those earlier years. And now – a photographer's paradise. Deregulation, to quote the PTE, has increased the bus miles operated and decreased the number of passengers carried. You hardly need to move from Piccadilly now to see as many operators in an hour as I would have seen all day forty years ago, but forty years ago, to quote one of Manchester's famous sons, 'they 'ad radiators n'mudguards'. So they did, and thank you for reminding me, Alan Beswick, for as we agreed on one of your breakfast book review slots, those *were* the days.

ACKNOWLEDGEMENTS

To do what you enjoy and be paid for it is the privilege of the few, so they tell me. To have the assistance and encouragement of friends and fellow enthusiasts at the same time is an added bonus. Many people have helped over the years in the gathering of material for this and other books. Forty years ago my neighbour and lifelong friend Alan Drabble was my constant companion on the many photographic excursions we made, almost always on our trusty bikes. Later Ken Sutton and Gwynne Thomas broadened my perception of what was going on behind the scenes.

Doug Jack opened many doors when Leyland was a builder of buses, instead of just another town in Lancashire. Eric Ogden has given considerable assistance with this work, doing most of the research for the captions and reading the proofs. Geoff Hyde tracked down some elusive dates whilst Keith Healey also did much delving for information and Geoff Lumb provided many of the early colour slides. These covered operators I had never photographed or others where my early films had not always stood the test of time. Finally Ken Swallow gave much encouragement and assistance and obtained invaluable material from Barrie Edwards which filled in gaps in the joint operation. Thank you all for your help, and I hope you enjoy the finished result.

Facing page
Ramsbottom's famous PD3, the last for the home market and the last half cab double-decker delivered to any of the PTEs, looks very smart in its GMT livery – basically a darker shade of orange and lighter white than that originally adopted by Selnec. New in November 1969 it was withdrawn from service in January 1981 and now resides in the Museum of Transport at Boyle Street, Manchester.

Right
Competition is to the fore in this illustration of the morning rush hour in Piccadilly. A GMBuses North Volvo single-decker, boldly emblazoned with its virtues for all to see, waits for the traffic lights to change whilst its rival slides quietly past en route to Altrincham, gaining an admiring glance from the lady passing by. Both bus and tram will compete for traffic on the section of the route between Bury and Manchester. The introduction of true low-floor buses by GMB (N) and other operators in November 1995 will radically change public transport in the city for up 'till then access for the disabled or those encumbered with push chairs and luggage was restricted to the Metrolink trams via their on-street platforms. The new high-tech buses will eliminate that advantage.

PHOTOGRAPHY

The photographs used in this book were taken by the Author, between May 1956 and November 1995, or are from the Senior Transport Archive, with the exception of the Charterplan picture, taken by Eric Ogden, and those on pages 8 (upper), 10, 11 (upper), 13, 14, 15, 16, 17, 18, 20, 22 (lower), 23, 25 (upper), 26 (upper right and lower left), 27, 31 (both upper), 32 (both), 33 and 34 (upper left) which were taken by Geoff Lumb. The maps were prepared by Mark Hughes and I record my grateful thanks to you all.

LOCATIONS

I have concentrated on the central area of the city for this photographic study. The area is more or less that which both Manchester Corporation and later GMT defined as the city centre in their maps and, starting from Deansgate Station – Knott Mill in 1956 of course – goes along Deansgate, taking in Bridge Street and King Street West, to Victoria including Greengate; Exchange Station approach; Victoria Station; Withy Grove; Great Ancoats Street; Newton Street; Piccadilly Station approach; Whitworth Street and Whitworth Street West back to Deansgate Station.

In 1956 the area within those boundaries was one which Alan Drabble and I regularly explored when we were not busy photographing further afield.

Several of the locations which provided rich pickings in 1956 have long since disappeared but the maps will assist those unfamiliar with Manchester of forty years ago.

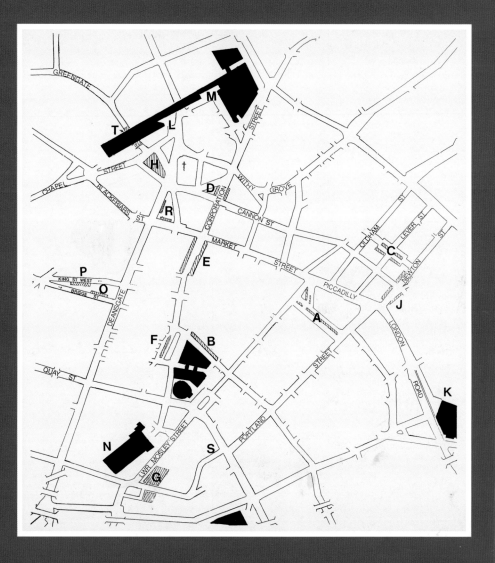

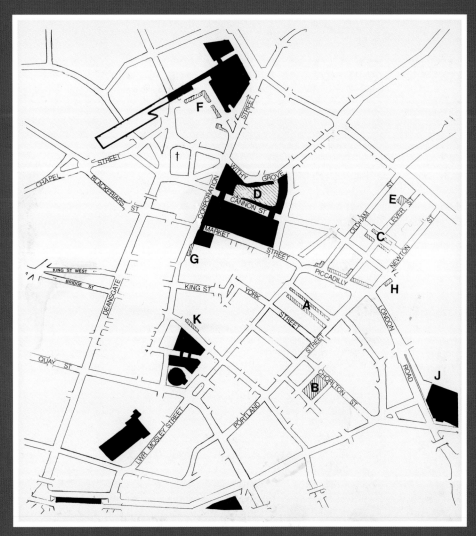

A	PICCADILLY BUS STN (PARKER ST)
B	PRINCESS STREET
C	STEVENSON SQUARE
D	CANNON STREET
E	CORPORATION STREET
F	ALBERT SQUARE
G	LOWER MOSLEY STREET
H	VICTORIA BDGE/ VICTORIA BUS STN
J	NEWTON STREET
K	LONDON ROAD STATION
L	EXCHANGE STATION
M	VICTORIA STATION
N	CENTRAL STATION
O	BRIDGE STREET
P	KING STREET WEST
R	ST MARYS GATE/ DEANSGATE
S	EAST STREET
T	GREENGATE

A	PICCADILLY
B	CHORLTON STREET
C	STEVENSON SQUARE
D	ARNDALE BUS STATION/ CANNON STREET
E	LEVER STREET BUS STATION
F	VICTORIA STATION
G	CORPORATION STREET
H	NEWTON STREET
J	PICCADILLY STATION
K	PRINCESS STREET

FORTY YEARS OF BUSES IN MANCHESTER

In 1956 Manchester city centre, through which I travelled to work, was a fascinating area for the bus enthusiast. Amongst the gleaming, brand new, Leylands, Daimlers and Guys could be found AECs, Albions, Atkinsons, Bedfords, Bristols, Crossleys, Dennises and even the occasional Foden. Virtually every week new vehicles were delivered to one or other of the operators serving the city, whilst old favourites faded quietly away. There were even new trolleybuses entering service! The city's buildings were grimy and black from blitz, smoke and fog, but its streets were kept clean.

The various bus stations or street stands in the centre regularly hosted a variety of operators – the municipalities whose vehicles worked jointly with Manchester's or Salford's transport departments; the two local BET operators, Ribble and North Western; two well-known independents, LUT and Maynes; and the various Tilling/BET/Municipal operators whose vehicles appeared on the Tyne-Tees-Mersey pool service, or the various express services including the legendary X60 to Blackpool. Some of the city's coach operators were regularly seen on my travels, as were the Scottish operators waiting in Lower Mosley Street after LRTA meetings at the Briton's Protection on the last Thursday of each month.

Public transport was the only way to and from work for most people and long queues were still an everyday feature of the evening rush hour, although motor car ownership was just coming to the shop floor workers – my journeyman had a Ford Anglia but the only other cars from the 30-strong workforce belonged to the boss, who ran a Daimler, his

son and the company secretary. Everyone else travelled by bus.

Victoria Bridge, the Victoria Bus Station and Greengate Arches were stretched to the limit at the peak. On Deansgate, St Mary's Gate and in Exchange Street buses unloaded and loaded in a never ending procession. Bridge Street and King Street West were also busy departure points. The map, overleaf, gives an indication of where those points were for the benefit of those who cannot remember the city before the big redevelopment at the bottom of Market Street.

Times were changing, that was obvious. One-man-operation (no women bus drivers in those days) and lightweight bodies were immediate signs of cost cutting – rear indicators started to be painted over in many fleets at this time. Simplified liveries came in with spray painting, lining out disappeared from most fleets, and fibreglass domes and wings made their appearance. The first were 'raw' on the inside, like Aero chocolate bars – Manchester had to fix metal straps, inside and out, on the front domes of its lightweight Orions to strengthen them.

Vehicles were generally still well turned-out and Salford manager Charles Baroth's 15 service from Worsley to Piccadilly could always be depended on to have extra-smart vehicles which, standing outside the Queens Hotel, would catch the eye of Manchester manager Albert Neal at 55, Piccadilly. A few years earlier representatives of every new batch appeared first on the 15; now, sadly those days had gone and all 195 8ft-wide Daimlers were virtually identical out of a fleet of 314. Mr Neal's day held no surprises in that quarter. I used the 15 for a change sometimes, one bonus was the chance to see what was inside

Weaste depot whilst the doors were open.

What was new ? Legislation was in hand to allow 2-axle double-deckers to be increased to 30ft long, matching Manchester, Ashton and LUT's 3-axle trolley buses. Air suspension was being talked about and Leyland were rumoured to have a completely new front-entrance rear-engined model in development and to be exhibited at the 1956 Motor Show. Increases in duty on fuel were causing serious problems for operators and fare increases were a fact of life.

Rush-hour congestion was rife, Market Street still handled two-way traffic, the Cheadle crawl was legendary and there was talk of an elevated dual-carriageway running – literally – right through my place of work. It duly became the Mancunian Way. Standee single-deckers were in vogue in some fleets and the underfloor-engined single-decker had effectively killed off the traditional front engined models.

Amongst the venerable old-timers, to be found in service or in non-revenue use, were some splendid canteens converted from Leyland Tigers and dating from the 'twenties which Manchester located in Cannon Street and Piccadilly. North Western responded with an ex-Rochdale ECW-bodied Leyland for crews at Lower Mosley Street. Piccadilly also had a tractor with padded buffer to help the reluctant starters on their way. Pre-war Leylands and Bristols abounded and wartime Guy utilities were still commonplace in many fleets.

North Western had undertaken a massive rebodying exercise on its numerous Bristols and Leylands and endless permutations of old chassis with new or second-hand bodies kept appearing from the Charles Street works in

Stockport. The bits left over went to Cowley, the local dealer, and could often be seen on the the waste land opposite the church at the foot of Blackfriars Bridge, before going to his other Manchester yard, or to Pennington. The huge Pennington yard was a sort of latter-day Aladdin's cave with vehicles from fleets I had only read about in *Buses Illustrated*.

In Lower Mosley Street we saw the long distance services, with express vehicles from Lancashire United, North Western, Ribble, Trent, West Yorkshire, Yorkshire Woollen District, and many other fleets. Round the corner in East Street were the coaches of Yelloway and Happiways, amongst others. I was always more interested in buses than coaches and for a while Sherry and Pendleton's ex-Salford pre-war Regents which could be seen there were more up my street. It was a good time to be busy with a camera, even if 120 size colour film was difficult to obtain and expensive to buy.

I vividly remember the end of South Lancashire Transport's venerable trolleybuses, and travelling on the last one from Farnworth with John Gillham on board, but then National Service intervened and introduced me to the coaches which operated from Piccadilly to the various military camps for 48-hour pass journeys. I never travelled on the splendid Silver Star coaches, being fated to use more mundane machines to Shropshire.

A spell 'down south' followed National Service and when we came back everything was changing. Selnec had arrived whilst we had been away and so the camera was busy again.

I have arranged this book in three parts. Firstly the scene as I saw it in 1956 and onwards, pure nostalgia as we look at all the old liveries and long-gone vehicles, though it hasn't proved possible to include everything in the 80 pages.

The second section covers the Selnec to GMT years when we came close to having a fully integrated transport system. Sadly the Thatcher Goverment had to interfere, botched it, and at a stroke managed to undo all the good work which had gone into years of co-ordination. Long before the National Lottery was conceived, splitting up the major operators created some instant millionaires; others had to wait a little longer. Competition has certainly been achieved but what a pity it doesn't get more people out of their cars and into all these empty buses.

And so the final section covers the scene as I saw it in 1995 – heatwave and all. The variety of liveries really does have to be seen to be believed – as does the state of some of the buses. Just as I was finishing off the final pages the Town Hall and PTE managed to pull off two master strokes which meant a little extra work was required. In a twin-pronged superbly-timed attack on the careworn bus station in Piccadilly and the polluted atmosphere in the city centre the two organisations closed the bus station for redevelopment and banned buses from travelling between the Arndale Bus Station and Piccadilly. I have to say it is now possible to cross the road much more easily but what those who rely on the buses to get to central Manchester will do remains to be seen. Doubtless the *Manchester Evening News* will tell us.

The pictures give an indication of what can be seen on a typical day by walking round the city centre, and show the multifarious liveries and vehicle types which once again grace the streets of Manchester.

'Everything was changing' – Victoria Bus Station

Ashton-under-Lyne Corporation PassengerTransport

First Corp tram	16/08/1902	Last tram	01/03/38
First t/bus	26/08/1925	Last t/bus	30/12/66
First m/bus	03/1923	Last m/bus	30/09/69

Ashton's buses were to be found in Piccadilly, along with its trolleybuses, and also in Lower Mosley Street bus station working the service 6 to Glossop, joint with Manchester and SHMD.

The livery for both buses and trolleybuses had changed in 1954 from the previous dark blue and white, lined in white and bright red, which dated back to tramway days. By 1956 the new livery of peacock blue and cream, as illustrated here and first applied to a trolleybus, was predominant, since many older vehicles had been withdrawn or rebodied and normal repainting was rapidly eliminating the earlier colours.

At this time the fleet consisted of 71 vehicles, 46 double-deck Crossley, Leyland and Guy, and 4 single-deck Leyland motor buses plus 21 double-deck trolleybuses of Crossley and Sunbeam manufacture. Ashton had just one depot which was closed in 1977 after the opening of the new Tameside garage by the PTE. For some while part of the original depot became a transport museum.

Joint stage carriage operation took Ashton's buses and trolleybuses to Manchester, while the buses also worked into neighbouring Glossop, Oldham, Rochdale, Stalybridge and Stockport. Operators with whom it operated jointly were North Western, Oldham, Manchester, Rochdale, SHMD and Stockport. There had also been joint operation with Salford before the war. Ashton had no coaches and operated no private hire though its vehicles were hired by others to work the X60 to Blackpool at peak holiday times.

The double-deck vehicle illustrated, 29, 229 YTB, a Roe bodied PD2, was photographed in Ashton's bus station in amongst SHMD and Manchester vehicles. The single-decker, 55, CTE 355E, was a Leyland Panther Cub, bodied by East Lancashire Coachbuilders. Although some wartime Guys had been rebodied by Bond in Manchester, Roe was Ashton's traditional body supplier.

Bolton's buses were to be found under Greengate Arches, Salford, and in Victoria bus station across the road, working the joint services 8 and 12 from Bolton.

The livery was still a dark maroon, with pale cream relief, which dated back to tramway days. In the 'sixties a lighter shade of red was applied, experimentally, as shown on the Orion bodied number 155. The arrival of Ralph Bennett saw a much brighter colour scheme applied, as shown on the fully-fronted PD3, using a lighter maroon than the original colour.

In 1956 the fleet consisted of 264 vehicles, 255 double-deck Crossley and Leyland, and 9 single-deck Crossley and Leyland. Bolton had three depots all of which were closed in 1979.

Joint stage carriage operation took Bolton's buses to Victoria, Salford, though they displayed Manchester on the blinds, while the buses also worked into neighbouring Bury, Leigh, Salford and Wigan. Operators with whom Bolton operated jointly were Bury, Leigh, LUT, Ribble, Salford and Wigan. Bolton had one committee coach which was very occasionally operated on private hire though its buses were regularly hired by others to work the X60 to Blackpool at peak holiday times.

The double-deck vehicle illustrated, 395, CWH 745, a Leyland-bodied PD2, was photographed with MCW Orion bodied PD2 155, SBN 755. The full fronted double-decker, 170, UBN 903, was a Leyland PD3, bodied by East Lancashire Coachbuilders. This batch of vehicles was purchased for use on the service to Southport, operated jointly with Ribble.

Bolton is not instantly thought of as a trolley bus operator but it owned four double-deck highbridge vehicles which were used on the Bolton-Leigh service and were operated and maintained by South Lancashire Transport from its Atherton premises. The four carried full SLT livery, with SLT logos, and not until their withdrawal when the SLT system closed, and their return to Bolton for sale to the breaker, did it become certain to the initiated just which four vehicles were Bolton's.

Bury Corporation Transport

First tram	1905	Last tram	02/1949
First t/bus	n/a	Last t/bus	n/a
First m/bus	1925	Last m/bus	30/09/69

Bury's buses were to be found in Cannon Street, by the Corn and Produce Exchange, working the joint service 35 from Bury.

The livery was pale green and pale cream, as shown. The earlier livery of red with pale cream relief, which dated back to tramway days, had gone by the 'fifties.

At this time the fleet consisted of 95 vehicles, 91 double-deck AEC, Crossley Daimler and Leyland, and 4 single-deck Roe-bodied Leyland PS1s. Bury had just one depot, and in the 'fifties it provided a home for former Newcastle tramcar number 102, now at the National Tramway Museum, Crich. The tram left Bury for Beaulieu around 1958.

Joint stage carriage operation took Bury's buses to Manchester, while the buses also worked into neighbouring Bolton, Ramsbottom and Rochdale. Operators with whom it operated jointly were Bolton, Ramsbottom, Rawtenstall, Ribble, Rochdale, Salford and Manchester. Bury had no coaches and operated no private hire though its vehicles were hired by others to work the X60 to Blackpool at peak holiday times.

The double-deck vehicle illustrated, 224, GEN 224, an MCW bodied Leyland PD3, typifies the livery and was photographed in the town centre. A similar vehicle is preserved in the Manchester Museum of Transport.

Lancashire United Transport Ltd			
First tram	n/a	Last tram	n/a
First t/bus	n/a	Last t/bus	n/a
First m/bus	1906	Last m/bus	01/04/81

Lancashire United's buses were to be found in Salford's Victoria bus station and under Greengate arches in addition to working express services through or from Lower Mosley Street.

The livery had recently changed from the original red and white, which dated back to tramway days, to a predominantly red with grey roof scheme, as shown, in 1950. The vehicles soon looked very drab and examples of the earlier livery remained in service until around 1957, several years after a third livery of all-over red with cream band had been introduced in 1951, as seen overleaf. Grey later replaced the cream relief for a while.

In 1956 there were 417 vehicles in the fleet; 242 double-deck of Daimler, Dennis, Foden, Guy and Leyland manufacture plus 175 single-deck Atkinson, Dennis, Guy and Leyland manufacture in use operating from depots in Swinton, Atherton, Platt Bridge (Wigan) with an outstation in Liverpool. Atherton remains in use in 1995, Swinton was closed in August 1991 and subsequently demolished for housing development, whilst Platt Bridge had been closed on 3rd March 1986.

Joint stage carriage operation brought Lancashire United's vehicles to Greengate, and Victoria bus station, Salford, again showing Manchester as the destination in both cases, and into neighbouring Bolton, Leigh, Salford, St Helens, Warrington, Wigan and Liverpool working jointly with Bolton, Leigh, Manchester, North Western, Ribble, Salford, St Helens, Warrington and Wigan, whilst express operation took the vehicles to Blackpool, Leeds, Liverpool, Middlesbrough, Morecambe and Newcastle.

Although dedicated coaches as such only joined the fleet in 1951, all single-deckers were classed as dual-purpose and could be found on private hire when required. The complexity of the company's operation and intensive use of vehicles resulted in workmen's services into Trafford Park being sometimes operated by the luxury coaches whilst express operation to Blackpool on the X60 could and frequently did see operation by early 'thirties lowbridge Leyland Titans. Variety was certainly the keynote for anyone interested in LUT's affairs.

The vehicle illustrated, 436, MTB 62, a Northern Counties-bodied Guy Arab III, was delivered in 1950 and withdrawn in 1966. It was photographed outside the workshops at Atherton after delivery from Northern Counties' factory in Wigan Lane, Wigan. The photograph enhances the livery which was quite drab out of the sun and much more so after a few months in service.

LUT (The Lancashire United Transport & Power Company until 1948) was Britain's biggest independent bus operator and its associate company, South Lancashire Transport Co, originally a tramway operator, ran a fleet of trolleybuses from the three depots mentioned. Suitably qualified crews worked on motor buses or trolleys as required, and in a fleet where vehicles had no traction batteries off-road manoeuvres with bamboo poles and long jump leads made for interesting spectator sports.

In tramway days the company generated its own power from a power station – out of sight to the left of the illustration, and also supplied many local homes and businesses. Nationalisation of the electricity industry in 1948 brought an end to this particular aspect of the company's business.

The upper photograph, taken outside LUT's Partington Lane, Swinton, depot shows the later livery applied to the half cab Guy coaches, the first true coaches to join the fleet. Number 443, MTJ 87, is shown. Bodied by Roe, for many years the company's principal single-deck supplier, they were delivered at a time when underfloor models were entering many other fleets. They appeared in all-over red with black trim to match the bus livery shown overleaf.

The Guy Arab IV double-decker alongside, 641, 358 FTB, with Northern Counties bodywork shows the later bus livery with cream relief band. The Daimler Fleetline, 183, PTE 633C, seen loading outside the depot in Partington Lane itself, carries the grey band. The common denominator in the LUT fleet was the choice of power unit, the Gardner engine. Business and family ties were strengthened when LUT Chairman Ned Edwardes' daughter Nora married one of the Gardner sons.

The Red Rose of Lancashire emblem can be seen on the front dash panel of the Fleetline and also the coach; it also appeared on the rear of many of the single-deckers. Examples of all three types of vehicle illustrated have been preserved and appear regularly at bus rallies in the north west and further afield.

In the 'seventies LUT adopted a livery which featured more grey and less red; some single-deckers were actually painted all-over grey, with a deep red band, without doubt the least attractive livery seen for many years but with the grey echoing the appearance of the very first buses and coaches operated by the company in the 'twenties.

Leigh Corporation Transport			
First tram	n/a	Last tram	n/a
First t/bus	n/a	Last t/bus	n/a
First m/bus	11/1920	Last m/bus	30/09/69

Leigh's buses were to be found only at Greengate arches, working the joint service 26 from Leigh.

The livery was blue and pale cream, as shown in the three illustrations. Two East Lancashire Coachbuilders-bodied AEC Renowns are shown in the upper view, PTC 115C carrying its Selnec number 6935 stands alongside ATE 190E. Lower left is Roberts-bodied AEC Regent III number 33, JTB 794, whilst lower right is Lydney-bodied Leyland PD2, KTD 759.

At this time the fleet consisted of 58 vehicles, 54 double-deck AEC, Guy and Leyland, and 4 single-deck Leylands. Leigh had just one depot which closed in February 1986. Its low roof height was one of the main reasons for the fleet being exclusively of lowbridge or lowheight configuration.

Joint stage carriage operation took Leigh's buses to Manchester, while the buses also worked into neighbouring Bolton and St Helens. Operators with whom it operated jointly were Bolton, LUT, Ribble, Salford and St Helens. Leigh had no coaches and operated no private hire though its vehicles were hired by others to work the X60 to Blackpool at peak holiday times.

For a small fleet Leigh managed to operate a selection of comparatively rare body makes. Its Lydney bodywork on Leyland Titans was unique in the Manchester area, as also was the Roberts bodywork shown. A Leigh Renown is preserved in the Manchester Museum of Transport.

13

Manchester Corporation Transport

First tram	07/06/01	Last tram	10/01/49
First t/bus	01/03/38	Last t/bus	31/12/66
First m/bus	1906	Last m/bus	30/09/69

Manchester's buses, naturally, were to be found throughout the city. They also worked into neighbouring Salford's Victoria bus station. The trolleybuses worked into Piccadilly and Stevenson Square.

The livery had remained virtually unchanged from the tramcar livery (itself inherited from the Manchester Carriage and Tramways Company), though the ivory gave way to pale cream in post-war years. By the mid-'fifties the amount of cream was being reduced and, in the fashion of the time, wings were being painted in the body colour rather than black as had previously been the case. A special blue and cream livery appeared on the rebuilt TS8 single-deckers allocated to airport duties in the early 'fifties and this was applied to new vehicles subsequently purchased for these services. It also appeared on some other batches used on non-airport duties.

In 1956 there were 1246 double-deck and 30 single-deck motor buses plus 190 double-deck trolleybuses. Crossley, Daimler and Leyland motor buses together with BUT, Crossley and Leyland trolleybuses were in use operating from depots at Hyde Road, Queens Road, Princess Road, Rochdale Road, Northenden and Parrs Wood..

Joint operation took Manchester's vehicles to Altrincham, Ashton, Bury, Glossop, Oldham, Rochdale, Stockport and Swinton. Joint operation was carried out with Ashton, Bury, North Western, Oldham, Rochdale, SHMD, Salford and Stockport. Manchester's coach seated vehicles were used for its prestige services but not for private hire or excursion work. Its more mundane vehicles appeared on the X60 and X70 from time to time, on hire to other operators.

The upper picture shows 3393, GNB 2, a 1940 Met-Cam bodied Leyland Titan TD5 photographed in Stevenson Square in 1955. Up to 1939 vehicles of this type had carried the streamline livery with pale cream swoops on both decks. In the background can be seen one of the then-new Burlingham bodied BUT trolleybuses. The lower illustration shows a Leyland PD2, number 3221, JND 622, with Manchester's post-war standard body. The smaller windows at the rear of both saloons are necessitated by the upper-deck body construction. To reduce damage in the event of a rear end collision Manchester opted to have the platform cantilevered from the upper deck, rather than attached to the chassis. In this way the chassis escaped damaged in minor accidents which could, nevertheless, do considerable damage to the platform and staircase area. Bodies to this style were built by Met-Cam, as here, and also by Brush and Crossley. Pre-war the window frames on both decks would have been ivory. Next came the livery shown above, then the cream on the upper-deck was eliminated. At this time roofs were grey on 7ft 6in wide vehicles, red on those which were built to 8ft., a useful indication for the men setting up the bus washers when such adjustments were required.

Of Manchester's garages Parrs Wood closed in April 71, Rochdale Road in August 1970, Birchfields Road and Northenden on Deregulation day. Hyde Road, Princess Road and Queens Road remain in use in 1995.

Manchester's blue livery was quite attractive and is seen here on one of its Leyland Tiger Cubs with Park Royal bodywork purchased in 1962 and in use on a one-man-operated service. Number 58, 3658 NE was in service for 13 years until 1975.

When Ralph Bennett introduced his Mancunian design, with its revised livery, greater use of the off white colour brightened up the fleet quite dramatically – as was the intention. One of the infamous rear-engined Panthers, No. 50, GND95E, is seen below in the single-deck version of the livery, working another o-m-o service. The vehicles were fitted with turnstiles to 'assist' boarding and the Tiger Cub's 'Pay as you enter' board has been replaced by the sign above the centre of the windscreen – the age of the logo was indeed upon us. Happily the long-established MCT bus stop has not yet shared the same fate.

Many of the Panthers managed only five or six years service and joined an ever increasing collection of fellow vehicles dumped at the back of Hyde Road works. An inspired piece of salesmanship saw many of these vehicles sold on to Australian operators – for whom they are reliably stated to have performed quite well. It was before the days when Foster's beer adverts might have suggested what the Aussie's reaction to these temperemental vehicles would be.

Manchester Corporation Transport

continued . . .

The new design of double-decker, introduced in 1968, carried a striking new livery as shown. The design was named the 'Mancunian', something of a far cry from earlier Mancunians with bulbous mudguards and boiling radiators, the latter streaked with rust and anti-freeze, which had been around a few years earlier. The location is the one-time George Street, site of a railway parcels office until the blitz, and now lost under the road realignment for Metrolink.

Number 1004, HVM904F, is a Leyland Atlantean PDR1/1 of 1968, with bodywork by Park Royal Vehicles Ltd to Manchester's striking design. It had a seating capacity of 73, with room for a further 23 standing passengers, and featured dual-doors. The new Selnec livery would not seem quite so avant garde when compared with this.

A Mayne and Son Ltd
First charabanc 1923   Last m/bus   extant

Mayne's buses were to be found in Lever Street and Stevenson Square, the nearest points to the city centre that the Corporation would allow them to reach. They ran to Droylsden via Ashton New Road and were the only independent to operate in competition with Manchester on its own territory. Between July 1958 and December 1966 Maynes operated jointly with Manchester on the 46 route from Droylsden to Stevenson Square.

The livery was maroon and turquoise, as shown.

At this time its fleet consisted of 22 vehicles, 11 double-deck AEC, and 11 single-deck Bedfords. Its depot was, and still is, situated on Ashton New Road.

Mayne's coaches operated on excursion and private hire work.

The illustration shows one of the stylish Neepsend-bodied AEC Regents delivered to the company in 1965, and photographed whilst loading in Stevenson Square.

North Western Road Car Co Ltd

First tram	n/a	Last tram		n/a
First t/bus	n/a	Last t/bus		n/a
First m/bus	1923	Last m/bus	01/01/72	

North Western's buses were to be found in Piccadilly, Cannon Street, Cateaton Street, Stevenson Square and Lower Mosley Street on a wide variety of services.

The livery was red and pale cream, as shown, but a major change in the application of the colours was taking place at this time. Spray painting was being introduced by many operators in the mid-'fifties but some of the benefits were reduced, or even lost, if complicated liveries were involved. Ribble was able to boast that it could spray a double-decker in 20 minutes, but simplified liveries were essential if such times were to be achieved. North Western changed from a livery which had used large areas of cream, including the roof, to the all-over red with cream relief seen here. It also briefly operated an unpainted vehicle, a Weymann-bodied Leyland single-decker, the only operator in the city to do so.

At this time its fleet consisted of 605 vehicles, 156 double-deck AEC, Bristol, Guy and Leyland, and 449 single-deck Atkinson, Bristol and Leylands. All its double-deckers were of lowbridge configuration except for one – the ex Rochdale ECW-bodied Titan which it used as a staff canteen at Lower Mosley Street. Its principal depot in the area was situated at Hulme Hall Road, alongside the railway at Cornbrook, whilst other depots were located at Altrincham, Glossop, Macclesfield, Northwich, Oldham, Urmston and Wilmslow. Hulme Hall Road is now Bee Line Bus Company's Manchester base. The main depot and head office were at Charles Street, Stockport. In 1961 there was a scheme to create a 130 space bus depot in the goods handling area below Central Station, now G-Mex, but nothing came of the proposal.

North Western's buses also worked into neighbouring Ashton, Eccles, Glossop, Oldham, Rochdale and Stockport in addition to towns further afield to which it operated Express services. Operators with whom it operated jointly were Ashton, Crosville, LUT, Manchester, Midland General, Oldham, PMT, SHMD, SJOC, Stockport, Rochdale, Trent and Warrington. North Western had a fleet of coaches and operated private hire work. Express operation took it to Barnsley, Blackpool, Leeds, Liverrpool, London, Middlesbrough, Morecambe, Newcastle, North Wales, Nottingham etc.

The illustration shows one of the pre-war Bristol Ks, 416, JA 7788, rebodied by Willowbrook in 1951/2, and seen outside the Norfolk Arms hotel in Glossop. This town, on the edge of the Peak District, had been an early point of entry for North Western's predecessor, British, with its dark green single deckers around 1920. The former North Western depot in the town is still in use in 1995.

The lower illustration shows number 394, EDB 321, an Atkinson single-decker, one of the first two taken into stock in 1951. Note that at this stage rear-entrance bodywork was still being purchased – there was no question of dispensing with the conductor.

17

More typical of North Western's single-deckers was this front entrance Leyland Tiger Cub, 672, KDB 672, one of large number with similar Weymann bodies on Royal Tiger and, later, AEC Reliance chassis.

The Fanfare Coach, 743, LDB 743, seen below left, marked a return to this sector of the market by Weymann. These bodies were found in North Western's fleet on AEC chassis, some examples being allocated to Altrincham Coachways and Melba Motors when these became NWRCC subsidiaries.

Later generations of single-deckers carried Alexander bodywork as seen below right and FJA 218D, an example with classic Y-type body was used on express work. It is fitted to a Leyland Leopard chassis. The Y-type body remained in production for 20 years, with only minor modifications in that time, and could be found throughout the country on AEC, Bristol and Seddon chassis.

Oldham Corporation Passenger Transport

First tram 15/12/1900	**Last tram**	03/08/46
First t/bus 26/08/25	**Last t/bus**	05/09/26
First m/bus /1923	**Last m/bus**	30/09/69

Oldham's buses were to be found in Stevenson Square, working the joint route 98 to Waterhead.

The livery was maroon and white, another instance of the tramcar livery being perpetuated, but in the late 'fifties/early 'sixties one vehicle was painted in two shades of blue, as shown, in an attempt to find a more attractive colour scheme. Municipal maroon, it seemed, had had its day. The blue scheme was not adopted but in its place a lighter red, known as pommard, was introduced. It lacked something of the robustness of the earlier colour. Note how on the blue livery the distinctive waist rail of the teak-framed Roe body, a patent in the design, has been highlighted to provide a contrasting stripe of yellow.

At this time the fleet consisted of 240 vehicles, 226 double-deck Crossley, Daimler and Leyland, and 14 single-deck Crossleys. It had just one depot which remains in use in 1995.

Oldham's buses could be found in neighbouring Ashton, and Rochdale. It operated jointly with Ashton, Manchester, North Western, Rochdale and SHMD, Oldham had no coaches and operated no excursion or private hire work.

The illustrations show three Leyland PD2s operated and photographed, below, whilst posed to demonstrate the two liveries. Roe bodied number 402, NBU 502, carries the very short-lived blue whilst 461, PBU 961, a Northern Counties example, wears the pommard which, after adoption, remained the undertaking's standard until Selnec days. In the larger illustration Roe-bodied number 394, NBU 494, the preserved example from Boyle Street, is taking a break between journeys whilst operating the Vintage Bus Service in Manchester's Heaton Park. It carries the original, darker maroon livery.

Oldham's Harry Taylor, instigator of these livery changes, was to play a very important part in the development of the Selnec Standard vehicles as will be explained later.

Rochdale's buses were to be found in Cannon Street and Stevenson Square, working the joint routes 8, 17, 24 and 90 to Rochdale.

It operated jointly with Ashton, Bury, Manchester, North Western, Oldham and Todmorden, and its vehicles could be found in neighbouring Ashton, Bury, Oldham and Todmorden. The livery was dark blue and pale cream, yet another instance of the tramcar livery being perpetuated, but in the late 'fifties/early 'sixties the livery was simplified and one of predominantly cream, with blue relief, was substituted. It did not seem to wear well and the former well-turned-out vehicles became quite drab in comparison with their earlier days.

In 1956 the fleet consisted of 155 vehicles, 140 double-deck AEC, Daimler and Leyland, and 15 single-deck AECs. It had just one depot, which was closed in August 1981.

Rochdale had no coaches and operated no excursion or private hire work.

Several of the industry's best-known managers spent time at Rochdale. George Cherry (1936-42) went on to serve for 22 years as general manager at Birkenhead. Chaceley Humpidge (1942-51) later did great things at Bradford and then Sheffield. Joe Franklyn (1951-1954), who helped Charles Baroth sort out Salford's problems, later went to be Manager at Blackpool for 20 years where his enthusiasm for the trams' capabilities was instrumental in their survival. And Ronald Cox (1954-62), also at Salford under Charles Baroth, later went to be manager at Edinburgh and then Director-General of Greater Glasgow PTE.

The illustrations show number 44, GDK 144, one of the Weymann-bodied AECs in the streamline livery and, below, number 7, HDK 707, one of the single-deck AEC Regals with East Lancs body showing how the all-cream livery was unsuited to Rochdale's environment.

Salford Corporation Transport			
First tram	10/1901	Last tram	31/03/47
First t/bus	n/a	Last t/bus	n/a
First m/bus	07/1920	Last m/bus	30/09/69

Salford's buses were to be found in Greengate, in the Victoria bus station, on Victoria Bridge Street, in Bridge Street and King Street West, in Piccadilly and in Cannon Street.

Salford operated jointly with Bolton, Bury, LUT, Leigh and Manchester. It had joint arrangements with, but did not operate with, North Western, Ribble, St Helens and Wigan. Its vehicles could be found in neighbouring Bolton, Bury, Leigh, and Reddish.

The livery was dark green and pale cream, replacing the original red and ivory of the trams and many other liveries which were left-overs from the war years, including greys and browns with or without the red. Salford was truly a Phoenix fleet and such was the state of the undertaking in 1946 that no one applied for the job of manager when John Blakemore finally retired. Charles Baroth eventually came, from Newport, very much on his terms, and did a magnificent, if autocratic job. His vehicles were always amongst the smartest in the area and the splendid breakdown vehicle, a Matador conversion of some style, was hardly ever seen out of its depot. No accident damage was ever seen on a vehicle in service.

In 1956 the fleet consisted of 324 vehicles, 313 double-deck AEC, Crossley, Daimler and Leyland, and 11 single-deck Daimlers. It had two depots, at Weaste and Frederick Road, the latter dating back to the start of municipal operation. Neither survives in use, Weaste being closed in January 1986 and is now used as a retail distribution warehouse whilst Frederick Road was closed on 26th October 1986, being subsequently demolished.

It had one coach, reserved exclusively for the use of the Transport Committee, and operated no excursion or private hire work.

The large illustration shows number 317, CRJ 317, one of the early post-war Leyland PD1s with Leyland bodywork. These originally had silver roofs but by 1956 roofs and wings were being painted green as shown. The small illustration shows the earlier red livery in its pristine glory. A feature of pre-war bus livery in Salford was the fascinating collection of information it embodied. Depot codes and allocation were perhaps surprising for a two-depot system but much more illuminating was the specific route allocation applied to some (not too many!) vehicles. Only the most mechanically reliable were allowed across the borough boundary on the longer joint workings.

This vehicle, BBA 560, and its fellow BBA 559, survived as dual-control driver trainers, renumbered 97 and 98, long after all other pre-Baroth vehicles had been despatched with great relief. BBA 560 survives in the Museum of Transport and was photographed when first restored, alongside the ornamental entrance to Frederick Road depot. The arch still stands in solitary splendour.

SHMD Joint Board			
First tram	10/1903	**Last tram**	05/1945
First t/bus	n/a	**Last t/bus**	n/a
First m/bus	/1925	**Last m/bus**	30/09/69

SHMD's buses were to be found in Piccadilly and Lower Mosley Street bus station.

They operated jointly with Ashton, Manchester, North Western, Oldham and Stockport and the vehicles could be found in neighbouring Ashton, Glossop, Oldham and Stockport.

The livery was dark green and pale cream, a carry-over from the trams, though with silver roof. Some vehicles had areas of lighter green relief. In the 'sixties a lighter shade of green was adopted overall and a simplified application of the livery took place at the same time. Vehicles carried the wording SHMD Board, or SHMD Joint Board, and, later, the splendid logo with the coats of arms of the four towns – Stalybridge, Hyde, Mossley and Dukinfield.

In 1956 the fleet consisted of 84 vehicles, 66 double-deck Atkinson, Daimler and Thornycroft, and 18 single-deck Atkinson, Daimler and Thornycroft. The Thornycrofts were rarely if ever seen in the city by this time, but the unique Atkinson double-decker was the source of much interest as it frequently came into Piccadilly on the joint working to Glossop. SHMD had the one depot, at Tame Valley, which was closed in 1977, making way for its brand new successor, itself to be closed at Deregulation on 26th October 1986.

It had no coaches, and operated no excursion or private hire work, though its vehicles regularly appeared in Blackpool on the X60 when hiring was necessary to cope with traffic.

The upper illustration shows NMA 335D, renumbered as Selnec's 5635, one of the Daimler Fleetlines, carrying Northern Counties bodywork as did all SHMD's buses, and painted in the lighter green. The lower illustration shows the earlier dark green livery on number 2, FTU 132, one of the pre-war Daimlers – with its distinctive bodywork – by then relegated to driver-training duties. The upper-deck front outline was an NCME hallmark for many years.

Stockport Corporation Transport

First tram	26/08/01	**Last tram**	25/08/51
First t/bus	10/03/13	**Last t/bus**	11/09/20
First m/bus	08/10/19	**Last m/bus**	30/09/69

Stockport's buses were to be found in Piccadilly, Albert Square and Princess Street. They operated jointly with Ashton, Manchester and North Western and SHMD, and the vehicles could be found in neighbouring Ashton and Glossop. The livery was bright red and white, again as used on the trams, with brown roofs.

In 1956 the fleet consisted of 168 vehicles, 148 double-deck Crossley, Guy and Leyland, and 20 single-deck Leylands. Stockport had no coaches, and operated no excursion or private hire work.

The illustration shows one of the locally-built Crossley DD42s with Crossley bodywork. Whilst the performance of the engine often left something to be desired the bodywork was always a first-class product. Number 322, EDB 576 is seen in its native town. Earlier double-deck vehicles had incorporated the Manchester design whereby the rear platform was cantilevered from the body structure but this batch was of conventional styling and construction.

South Lancashire Transport			
First tram	21/10/02	Last tram	16/12/33
First t/bus	03/08/30	Last t/bus	31/08/58

Ashton under Lyne Corporation PassengerTransport			
First t/bus	26/08/25	Last t/bus	30/12/66

Manchester Corporation Transport Department			
First t/bus	01/03/38	Last t/bus	30/12/66

In 1956 there remained but three of the trolleybus systems which had operated in the Greater Manchester area, with a selection of types of South Lancashire Transport, Ashton and Manchester Corporation vehicles.

There had been trolleybuses in Oldham, Ramsbottom, Stockport and Wigan, in addition to the early Ashton trolleybuses but with the exception of Ashton all these 'first generation' systems had closed by 1930 when the South Lancs system opened.

In 1956 Ashton and Manchester trolleybuses could still be seen in the city centre but the nearest point where South Lancashire vehicles could be seen was Swinton. Because of the venerable age of the vehicles and the nature of the system it is included in this book, even though it falls outside the strict geographical limit defined at the beginning.

The South Lancashire Transport Company's trams were withdrawn beginning in 1930 and total conversion to trolleybus operation was complete by December 1933. This system was operated entirely by two and three-axle double-deckers initially of Roe-bodied lowbridge configuration on Guy chassis. Later chassis were of Leyland manufacture followed by wartime Karrier/Sunbeams and post-war Karriers. From 1934 all vehicles were of highbridge pattern.

Trolleybuses belonging to the South Lancashire Transport Company were operated from all three depots belonging to sister company Lancashire United Transport. A particularly interesting aspect of the system was its occasional use by Leyland Motors for the testing of prototypes and also pre-delivery testing of customers' vehicles under the SLT wires.

There were four main routes, the rambling Farnworth to Atherton via Swinton; Atherton to St. Helens; Leigh to Bolton; Atherton to Mosley Common. The first to be abandoned was the St. Helens route, operated jointly with that undertaking's trolleybuses, which became something of a hot potato when it was withdrawn on November 11th 1956, during the Suez crisis, at a time when petrol and diesel fuels were temporarily rationed following the closure of the Suez Canal.

The photograph on the opposite page shows number 1, the original vehicle which was used to train tram drivers for the conversion in 1930, standing at Swinton Church. In the background a Manchester Corporation Crossley waits to depart on service 57 to Reddish, jointly operated with Salford. There had been proposals before the war to make this and the 77 route, which operated anti-clockwise around Pendlebury to reach the Swinton terminus, a trolleybus route but in the event the 210, as it became, operated only from Piccadilly. Salford never operated trolleybuses, of course.

The final night of operation was on 31st August 1958 though specially repainted number 71, the last vehicle purchased, carried local dignitaries to a function the following day, being specially licensed for the event and as such being LUT's only trolleybus since the SLT company had ceased to exist at midnight on the 31st August.

In 1956 Ashton operated 32 trolleybuses, again of two and three-axle configuration, all highbridge double-deckers, from its single depot in the town. Routes were operated from Ashton to Manchester and Ashton to Haughton Green. A keen advocate of the trolleybus it had rebodied some of its earlier vehicles, including wartime models, but was obliged to close the system when Manchester decided to abandon its system. Ashton's last trolleybus ran on the night of 30th December, 1966. The illustration shows a two-axle Crossley bodied Crossley vehicle.

Manchester's trolleybuses operated routes from Piccadilly and Stevenson Square to Ashton, Haughton Green and Gee Cross and from Miller Street to Greenheys. In 1956 there were 116 remaining in service, the original 76 pre-war vehicles having been withdrawn. Forced upon a reluctant Stuart Pilcher by his Committee in 1938 they operated from two depots, Hyde Road and the purpose-built Rochdale Road garage which was used by motor buses after the trolleybuses were withdrawn, being later closed when the motor bus fleet size reduced with cutbacks.

All vehicles were double-deck highbridge, with two or three axle Leyland and Crossley or two axle BUT chassis, and Metro-Cammell, Burlingham or Crossley bodywork. The last service trolleybus ran on the same night as Ashton's, 30th December, 1966. On the following day special arrangements allowed the operation of two preserved trolleybuses, one ex-Manchester and the other from Rotherham, to run an enthusiast's tour. The photograph shows a Burlingham-bodied BUT example from the last batch of trolleybuses purchased by Manchester waiting to depart from the Portland Street terminus in Manchester's Piccadilly.

With the closure of these two systems Manchester remained without electric traction on its streets until the arrival of the Metrolink trams in 1992.

Ribble Motor Services Ltd

First m/bus	06/1919	Last m/bus	31/12/68
To NBC	01/01/69	Privatised	03/88
To Stagecoach Holdings Ltd			04/89

Ribble Motor Services, based at Frenchwood Avenue, Preston, operated into Lower Mosley Street Bus Station, which, owned by Omnibus Stations Ltd, was a Mecca for enthusiasts, particularly at weekends and Bank Holidays when a never-ending stream of vehicles came and went. The new Concert Hall, home of the Halle Orchestra, now stands on one half of the site, whilst the other is still derelict at the time of writing.

The list of operators whose vehicles could be seen on a Bank Holiday weekend was legion for, in addition to the long list of 'regulars', there came the hired-in buses and coaches from other local operators. The X60 service to Blackpool alone would provide a who-was-who of the area. Sadly all has now gone and it is difficult for today's enthusiasts to appreciate just how much more interesting it was than its successor Chorton Street for, as the pictures show, the area was open and readily accessible for photography. Access to the west side was from Albion Street via Trumpet Street, and there was a single vehicle outstation depot where one Ribble bus could be housed overnight as required.

Captions to facing page

The changing face of Ribble's buses in Manchester

Upper left: Ribble's White Ladies were regular visitors to Lower Mosley Street and their attractive colour scheme meant that they stood out amongst the other, more drab, vehicles of the day. Although of lowbridge configuration they had heaters and rear doors and proved popular at a time when for many people they were the only means of getting to the seaside. On a more mundane but very important level they also provided daily transport to work, of course, operating on the east Lancashire services to Clitheroe and Burnley. Leyland PD2s, they were bodied by Burlingham, or as here, East Lancashire Coachbuilders.

Lower left: The second-generation White Ladies were Metro Cammell Weymann-bodied Leyland Atlanteans, some of which were equipped with toilets as in the case of the vehicle illustrated. Note the reversed livery, using the standard Ribble colours of the time.

Lower centre: Later vehicles purchased for use on Express services were full-fronted buses bodied either by Burlingham or MCW. They were fitted to Leyland PD3 chassis and had forward entrances. They were large and impressive vehicles in their attractive Cherry Red livery.

Lower right: After the formation of the National Bus Company Ribble's buses started to appear in the washed-out Poppy Red livery. With the passage of time it seems somehow less unattractive nowadays but when compared with Ribble's lovely Cherry Red it was a very poor substitute at the time. An MCW-bodied Atlantean waits in Lower Mosley Street before setting off to Clitheroe.

Upper right: A dual-purpose Leyland Leopard with BET style Marshall bodywork, in the same place. The east Lancashire services operated from this part of the bus station.

Sheffield Joint Omnibus Committee vehicles were seen on Manchester's Exchange Station approach, operating the 48 service to Sheffield via the Snake Pass. The Willowbrook-bodied Leyland Leopard, 1017, 617 BWB, seen upper right is typical of the allocation in the mid-'fifties.

Lower Mosley Street bus station was the arrival and departure point for the long-distance services operated by Tilling and BET companies, and also the local service number 6 to Glossop, jointly operated with vehicles from Ashton, North Western SHMD and Manchester. In addition to the Ribble and North Western vehicles already illustrated the Northern Pool service from Liverpool to Leeds and Newcastle together with other express services into Yorkshire, east Midlands and Scotland provided a host of operators – Lancashire United, Northern General, Potteries Motor Traction, Trent, United, Western SMT, West Yorkshire, Yorkshire Traction, Yorkshire Woollen District, and even the occasional Crosville on hire.

The centre illustration shows a Trent Willowbrook-bodied Leopard of the type common on the service from Manchester to Nottingham, though actually seen in Stockport. In the early to mid'fifties Trent, Ribble and North Western's Leyland Royal Tigers with Leyland 41-seat central-entrance bodywork were much in evidence on such express workings.

No book including express services in-and-around Manchester would be complete without a mention of Hubert Allen's famous Yelloway company, thriving in 1956 but now sadly no more. A long-standing AEC user the Yelloway fleet was always immaculate and passengers in Manchester were picked up and set down in East Street coach station, behind Lower Mosley Street with access further round Chepstow Street. Happiways and Spencers, amongst others, also used East Street but after its closure Yelloway coaches picked up from Central Station forecourt. The illustration shows a line of Yelloway Harrington-bodied AEC Reliance coaches at the Weir Street, Rochdale, headquarters.

1969 – FORMATION OF THE PTEs CREATES **SELNEC** AND, LATER, GMT IN MANCHESTER.

Selnec P.T.E.
Peter House
Oxford Street
Manchester M1 5AW

The ten years from 1956 saw continuing change through the Manchester area as operators eliminated the last of their pre-war stock, and underfloor engined single-deckers were seen everywhere; by this time the troublesome rear-engined double-deckers were gradually becoming accepted in most fleets. Manchester was taking delivery of its new Mancunian double-deckers, a bold imaginative design evolved between Ralph Bennett, the new MCTD Manager, Ken Mortimer, the resident designer-cum-PR man, and Park Royal Vehicles Ltd.

Electricity played a smaller part in the area's transport than many felt was wise, especially with the unsettled situation in the Middle East whence our oil supplies came. The SLT trolleybus system had closed in 1958 and the Manchester and Ashton systems had only a few months left to run, both being scheduled to close in 1966. The diesel bus, and to some extent train, reigned supreme.

Although most operators were modifying their liveries to make cost savings the modifications generally amounted to little more than elimination of some of the cream bands and the introduction of spray painting. Advertising was more widespread and all-over-advertising was making its presence felt on double-deckers. Yellow Pages were early in this field and their

place in posterity was assured when Dinky Toys produced a toy Atlantean double-decker in Yellow Pages colours.

Buses generally looked quite smart, usually more so in the smaller fleets, and there was plenty of variety for the observer. Lower Mosley Street Bus Station offered a good selection of long distance operators' vehicles, with Ribble prominent but North Western, Trent, West Yorkshire, Yorkshire Woollen District, Yorkshire Traction, Western SMT and others livening up the scene.

In 1968 Barbara Castle's Transport Act set out, amongst other aims, to try to improve life in the cities, and elsewhere, by encouraging people to travel by public transport. Believing that big-is-beautiful the Labour Government decided to create a Nationalised bus company – NBC – and to introduce Passenger Transport Authorities to be responsible for transport in the major conurbations, of which Manchester was one.

The formation of the PTE's, the operating arms of the PTA's, meant the elimination of the glorious mix of colours from the various municipal fleets. Manchester had a long tradition of joint operation, or through running, going back to tramway days in the early years of the century. Reduction of dead mileage and inter-availability of tickets and timetables were just two advantages. Both were retained under the new arrangements but eventually

the ten local authority liveries disappeared, as also did North Western and LUT's liveries, gradually, from 1974 and 1976 when they also were drawn into the net. It took some time for civic pride to be eliminated; pre-Selnec colours could still be seen in 1982, fourteen years after the orange and white first appeared.

As if this wasn't bad enough the formation of NBC resulted in the virtual loss of identity of the former Tilling and BET fleets when they were all painted in the standard NBC colour schemes – Poppy Red for the former 'red' companies, Leaf Green for the former 'green' companies, and white for the express vehicles and coaches. Gradually the traditional cherry red and Tilling red and greens disappeared, along with all the other well-loved colour schemes so long a part of Manchester's rich transport heritage.

For some years the variety in types of buses and their colours increased, some vehicles being repainted into orange and white whilst others of the same batch remained in their original colours, albeit renumbered and without their original municipal crests. That period is recalled in these two pages, with examples from the former fleets and new deliveries showing the new corporate livery.

Facing page:

The Selnec lazy S appeared in Orange, Blue, Magenta, Green and Brown over the years prior to the change to the GMT logo.

Vehicles on order for the former constituents arrived in Selnec colours but their style and detailing often immediately showed for whom they had been intended. If that wasn't obvious then the registration numbers usually settled it. Salford had ordered a batch of Mancunians, but fitted with its standard destination layout and with seats finished in Salford's usual green vinyl covering. SRJ 329H, Selnec 1206, leaves Victoria Bridge Street for Walkden on Salford's route 9 in 1971. This was a busy bus terminus, having previously also served as a tram terminus, and was supported by the bus station below as shown on page 5. The Grosvenor Hotel, behind the bus, gives a reminder of just how dirty many of the city's building still were at that time though the Grosvenor was lucky to be there at all, the entire block facing it on the other side of Deansgate having been destroyed in the blitz.

SHMD seemed particularly determined to hang on to its green livery and also found the application of the Selnec divisional flashes could be applied quite neatly and unobtrusively. Stockport was similarly minded but authority in the Divisional Office was not impressed and an edict was issued that the transfers must be applied on a large white background panel. The result was an undescribably awful eyesore which clearly showed that lack of taste and appreciation for the finer points of presentation were not understood in some quarters at least. Here Leyland Titan 5687, 87 ETU, loading in Ashton bus station before returning to Lower Mosley Street Bus Station, Manchester, on one of the area's most interesting jointly-operated routes shows how neat the first version looked on the stylish Northern Counties body.

Colourful liveries in early Selnec days. A former Ashton Corporation Roe-bodied Leyland Titan, now without its municipal markings, is seen prominent in the right foreground, waiting its turn to move to the traffic lights whilst leaving room for a former SHMD Bristol RE, with NCME bodywork and now sporting Selnec colours to cross over into Ashton's bus station which is out of sight on the left. Last in the line of three double-deckers held by the traffic lights is a North Western Park Royal-bodied AEC Renown, still owned by NWRC in this 1971 view. Beyond is a former Salford City Transport Daimler Fleetline with MCW bodywork, operating the joint service 64 to Peel Green and still wearing its original green and cream livery. Waiting at the lights a former Stockport Corporation Leyland Titan, with East Lancashire Coachbuilders bodywork in the distinctive Stockport livery of red and white prepares to return to its native town.

Facing page

Top left: Locally built Seddons with Pennine bodywork were initially purchased to be used on the more lightly trafficked routes and also on the inter-station service. Later the Dennis Dominos replaced them. Number 1707, XVU 337M, is seen here in Selnec colours with the orange Selnec flash.

Top right: One of Leigh's lowbridge Leyland Titans, 493 DTC, now 6957, in this case with bodywork by East Lancashire Coachbuilders, is carrying the Magenta flash of the Northern division.

Lower left: A former SHMD Daimler Fleetline with Northern Counties bodywork, NMA 327D, now number 5627, carries the green flash of the Southern division. The left hand street light behind the vehicle is mounted on a traction pole from the former trolleybus turning loop at Hyde's Gee Cross, still the terminus of the 210 service from Piccadilly as can be seen.

Lower right: Not quite what it seems. TWH 809K, 6809, a former Bolton Atlantean with East Lancashire Coachbuilders bodywork and carrying GMT darker orange livery and logos swings round with a full load in Halifax during an enthusiasts day based on the Piece Hall in that town. The vehicle is one of many former Selnec or GMT vehicles now preserved and splendidly restored.

Ramsbottom Corporation Transport

First tram	n/a	Last tram	n/a
First t/bus	14/08/13	Last t/bus	31/03/31
First m/bus	/1923	Last m/bus	31/10/69

Two Greater Manchester municipal operators which did not run into the city centre were Ramsbottom Urban District Council and Wigan Corporation, but since both eventually became part of the GMT fleet they are included here for completeness.

The Ramsbottom fleet of twelve buses, housed in the Stubbins depot, was the smallest of the eleven which formed the Selnec PTE operation in November 1969. This Ramsbottom order was delivered to Selnec in that month in full council livery of maroon and pale cream but was eventually repainted in Selnec orange and white as seen on page 2.

The UDC's main services were between Rawtenstall and Bury via Ramsbottom, and surrounding villages were served. Number 11, the last front-engined Titan, is shown here numbered 6411 in the Selnec fleet on service between Bury and Edenfield. It was withdrawn in 1981 and restored to its original livery before entering Boyle St. museum.

Wigan

First tram	25/01/01	Last tram	28/03/31
First t/bus	07/05/25	Last t/bus	30/09/31
First m/bus	09/06/19	Last m/bus	31/03/74

Wigan remained a municipal operator until 1974, when local government reorganisation brought the fleet into the newly formed GMPTE, the successor to Selnec PTE. It had one depot, in Melverley Street. The livery was a deep madder and white.

Number 27 was one of a batch of nine Leyland Titans delivered to Wigan in 1968. Bodywork was by the local company, Massey Bros Ltd, and 1968 was the last year of production.

Wigan No. 27, FEK 3F, was photographed in the town centre in Corporation days. Together with the other members of the batch it was repainted in GMT livery, being numbered finally 3292. Most of the batch worked from Oldham depot and all were withdrawn in 1981, whereupon No. 27 passed to a driving school in Sheffield. Notice the twin green lights on either side of the destination panel, a feature retained to the end by Wigan Corporation. Another Wigan Titan, also with forward entrance bodywork by Massey, survives the time of writing in the Greater Manchester Buses South driving school fleet based at Hyde Road. It is the only remaining front-engined double-decker in either of the GMB fleets.

Selnec inherited a wide variety of bus makes and types upon its formation. Some 2,340 double-deckers and 174 single-deckers, on nine chassis makes and carrying more than double that number of body manufacturers products passed into its empire and there was obviously a need to standardise as soon as possible. The decision was taken to purchase Leyland Atlantean and Daimler Fleetlines as the basis of the standard double-deck fleet, and a body design was evolved in consultation with Park Royal Vehicles, builders of the Bennett Mancunian body for Manchester, and Northern Counties, the Wigan based company which had been but a minor supplier to Manchester up until that time.

Early Atlantean chassis had many problems and the engineers from the PTEs, led by Harry Taylor from GMPTE, spent much time and effort in working with Leyland to improve the reliability of the vehicle. The outcome was an improved model, coded AN68.

Atlantean 7001, the first production standard, is seen here with its PRV bodywork . It followed 21 prototypes from Northern Counties, all numbered in the EX series of experimental vehicles. The initial production bodies came from PRV but Northern Counties examples soon appeared. There were obvious differences mainly in the front dome and rear upper-deck bay treatment but otherwise they were externally very similar and all examples looked very smart in the new Selnec orange and off white livery. Unfortunately this did not weather well. Over the years the livery has benefited from a progressive darkening of the shade of orange. Small numbers of vehicles were built with two-door configuration bodywork but this soon fell from favour.

The design remained in build to the end of Atlantean and Fleetline deliveries, with vehicle number 8765 in 1984 and was then modified by the thickening of the pillar at the rear of the first upper deck bay to suit the longer front overhang of the Olympian and in that form has also been used on Scania and Dennis chassis. Following a wholesale withdrawal of buses by GMT at Deregulation several hundred were offered for sale and examples of the former style can still be seen with many operators in Manchester, including Bee Line, Bullocks, Finglands, Maynes, South Manchester, and Walls in addition to the GMB fleets. They can also be seen in many other parts of the country. Number 7001 now resides in the Boyle Street Museum of Transport.

THE SELNEC STANDARD DOUBLE-DECK BUS

SELNEC CHESHIRE

On New Year's Day 1972 North Western's bus mileage within Selnec's area passed to the PTE, along with five depots and 272 buses. Other former North Western vehicles went to National Travel North West and Crosville. The familiar red and cream livery lasted for some while but from March 1972 the Selnec logo began to appear, in brown, as seen below. Soon the full Selnec livery appeared, as shown right, in later years, on a Renown carrying GMT logos and photographed outside Glossop's Norfolk Arms terminus of the former joint number 6 service, now 236. Below left is one of North Western's Alexander bodied Fleetlines with Selnec Cheshire logo and all-over advertising livery outside Bennett Street Parcel depot during an open day at Hyde Road works whilst right is a similar Fleetline which passed to Crosville, seen in Piccadilly.

LANCASHIRE UNITED

Lancashire United's red and grey buses finally fell to the PTE in 1976 but no immediate change was apparent to the casual observer. The three depots remained in use, as did the workshops and offices at Atherton. The workshops, seen behind the bus in the upper picture, once formed the depot for the trams and, later, the trolleybuses of the SLT fleet. An interesting feature was a traverser at the far end of the building which incorporated a turntable, thus allowing trolleybuses to enter and leave in clockwise fashion and to change 'roads' as required.

Not until 1978 did the Lancashire United company, Britains's biggest independent, become fully integrated within GMT and the familiar orange and cream livery then began to appear on vehicles from the former Atherton based company, though it was not applied in the same proportions as the rest of the fleet. Because LUT had long standardised on Northern Counties bodies, and had adopted the Manchester style destination display in the 'fifties when Mr Oakham was the Manager, many of its later double-deckers had more than a passing resemblance to the GMT standard vehicles. In fact there were several significant differences, including LUT's preference for engine compartment shrouds, 33ft long vehicles and dual-doorway bodywork. The upper photograph shows number 412, VTC 502M, to LUT specification and newly delivered to Atherton from NCME, waiting to make its first journey later that day, though not on the 41 service. From 1977 GMT standards began to enter the fleet, but in LUT grey and red livery.

More interesting to the enthusiast, perhaps, was the Guy element of the LUT fleet, for there were still no less than 140 Arab IV and V models in every day use and still being seen in Manchester on a regular basis. Happily several of these have survived in preservation and another significant part of Manchester's transport history has been kept alive.

A former LUT Plaxton bodied Leopard, seen below, seems set to be one of if not the last vehicle from a pre-Selnec fleet still in revenue service with one of the GMB fleets, in this case GMB North. Ordered by LUT at a time when the Bristol REs it wanted were no longer available to it, and the National was seen as unacceptable, it has given good service and was photographed whilst rallying in 1995 at the Piece Hall in Halifax.

DEREGULATION COMES TO MANCHESTER

By the 1980s the former multi-coloured scene in Manchester had become somewhat muted, and many of the interesting vehicles which had passed to Selnec from the constituent fleets had been withdrawn. All was not lost, however, since the politicians were about to bring more variety to the scene than anyone could ever have imagined.

The Selnec – later GMT – orange and white livery was to be seen everywhere throughout Greater Manchester. The shade of orange had been darkened, brown (later black) skirts were applied to the double-deckers, but it was still a very uniform image, as indeed it was intended to be. It always seems to be the case, however, that with any major change of livery in large fleets no sooner has the job been completed, and all vehicles are in one corporate scheme, than some bright spark sets the whole scene rolling again with another new colour scheme.

The next change in liveries was triggered off in a different way, however, in 1986 when the deregulation of the whole bus industry resulted locally in a change unprecedented in Manchester's history and one which swept through the streets as an ever-increasing number of operators brought their many and different coloured buses into competition with the Greater Manchester Buses Ltd two-thousand strong fleet.

Following the Government's decision to introduce competition to the bus industry this wholesale change occurred in public transport through the country, apart from London where the Government decided that the risks of letting the world see its policy in action in Parliament Square were perhaps too great; certainly the

Left:
'a modern fleet in a corporate and attactive livery'. Piccadilly c1975.

Facing page:

Piccadilly 1995 – only the Metrolink articulated tram shows any evidence of investment; the buses could well have been amongst those which had been photographed on the other side of the bus station twenty years earlier, as seen left.

result would be no vote catcher if Manchester's experience is anything to go by.

Many people had been sceptical of Selnec, and later GMT. The feeling that the municipalities had always done a good job and, generally, operated efficiently, was still evident. Nevertheless there were clear benefits to be seen on the streets, with a modern fleet in a corporate and quite attractive livery, fully integrated through a vast area around Manchester.

Unfortunately, as is always the case, a very small number of individuals can spoil any large organisation and some of the drivers employed were, to put it kindly, totally unsuited to their work. Their cavalier attitude stemmed from a feeling that they were fireproof in an organisation controlled by a strong left-wing council. The economics of the Deregulated world passed them by as they upset their passengers and often brought down the wrath of the public on the whole organisation.

This was a tragedy for it played into the hands of those who insisted that unrestricted competition was the answer to this and all other problems. Small comfort for them that things have not always improved, certainly not in the age of the buses on the streets or their ability to create clouds of noxious fumes.

Fortunately though, there has been a recognition that bus drivers do need to be trained in their attitude to people and most drivers at last realise that very often those passengers who find their attitude off-putting now have a choice of operator, and that passenger's fares actually pay driver's wages.

The immediate effect of deregulation was a wholesale withdrawal of several hundred buses from the GMT fleet. These were lined up awaiting purchasers in long rows in three GMT garages which had also been made redundant. Such were the numbers involved that the PTE set up a selling organisation with Kirbys (the coach dealers) to dispose of the vehicles.

Because of the uncertainties of the effects of this very different operating situation orders for new vehicles throughout the country fell to disastrously low levels and long-established bodybuilders throughout the UK fell one by one. Park Royal had already been closed, in 1980, but the collapse in confidence and resulting lack of orders for new buses meant that the principal double-deck suppliers to GMT were at risk. The MCW organisation ceased building buses in 1989 and even Northern Counties, then owned by the PTA, was not immune; it passed into Official Administration during 1991, though happily it has survived.

The large numbers of Standard Atlanteans and Fleetlines, with modern bodywork and no shortage of spares, soon found buyers and very soon after Deregulation Day in October 1986 they began to reappear on Manchester's streets, in new liveries. The numbers of former GMT employees made redundant by the reduction in fleet size should have been clear warning of the effects of the spread of competition but it still took some time for the message to come through to some platform staff. Several former employees bought buses, however, and began to operate amongst the competition.

Anybody with an Operator's Licence can now operate buses on any route, though the Traffic Commissioner still looks at applications for new routes. Operators can withdraw from a route by giving 42 days notice. A previously unimaginable situation has now arisen, however, whereby a service can have one

operator during daytime, Monday to Friday; another in the evenings; usually one of these two on a Saturday and possibly a third operator or no operator at all on a Sunday. Integration and commonsense, it would appear, were both removed simultaneously.

Those who do not travel on buses, having instead the use of a car and chauffeur to travel around London or elsewhere on government business, clearly have no conception of the situation where a passenger may not know which operator's bus is the one he or she should be attempting to flag down unless they regularly use the service. It gives little incentive to the occasional would-be passenger to change to using public transport.

Quite apart from its more serious effect on passengers and operators, post-1986 also became a time of challenge for the observer and recorder alike as companies came and went, and vehicles were sold from one operator to another. Even some examples of the famous London Routemaster made an appearance in Manchester, running in competition with everyone else on the much vaunted yet still-profitable Wilmslow Road corridor.

And there lay the problem, for everyone wanted to operate commercially on the profitable routes whilst the non-profitable ones had to be put out to tender for a subsidised service, if indeed anyone wanted to take them on.

Thus some areas are flooded with buses, whilst others are starved. This is a long-running bone of contention for would-be passengers in the badly-served areas and a regular flow of letters to the Manchester Evening News highlights this fact. The PTE responds by pointing out that it no longer has control – *"The Authority would like to see a return to a situation where we regulate bus services to prevent these problems."* said Councillor Jack Flanagan in response to such a letter recently.

Another bone of contention for some people has been light rail in Manchester. Whilst Metrolink would always be controversial because of the amount being spent on a system providing for only a small percentage of the Greater Manchester population it hardly made sense to invest £112m plus in the Light Rail Scheme, then encourage all-and-sundry to compete with it, and then to complain that air pollution was reaching dangerous levels. The platitudes of Roger Freeman from the Department of Transport did little to help when he assured everyone that Deregulation was clearly good for Manchester and was working well. Working well for whom?

Gradually order is coming out of the chaos and at last investment is becoming apparent in the form of a steady intake of new buses. The recognition that modern, clean and comfortable vehicles staffed by well-trained cheerful professional drivers encourage passengers has brought about a long-awaited and much-needed improvement.

A particularly welcome move has been made by the PTE whereby operators who purchase new generation low-flow buses such as the Wright-bodied Axcess single-deckers can obtain a substantial cash rebate towards the purchase price. In this way the PTE demonstrates it

High profile:
Oldham Street's busy junction with Piccadilly provides a never-ending stream of buses of all shapes, sizes and colours.

Low profile:
The Dominos have been moved away from their previous spot at the top of the station approach to a location nearer to the main concourse of Piccadilly Station, but tucked away from sight of the stranger to Manchester.

continuing commitment to improving the standard of service and ease of access for all passengers, thereby helping to encourage people to use public transport.

Notwithstanding these positive aspects the ability of some large bus companies to operate profitably has generated new, large and very powerful groups, making a mockery of the whole Thatcher policy of 'small is beautiful' and 'there shall be competition' when her policies have forced the split of GM Buses and, earlier, NBC and its larger subsidiaries such as Ribble and Crosville.

However, if transport enthusiasts walking the streets of Manchester give any thought to politicians they would probably relate more to Harold MacMillan, if they remembered him, for indeed the *'wind of change'* has swept though the industry, and the observer and photographer have certainly *'never had it so good'* in terms of colour and variety of models.

At its ridiculous peak there were some 60 plus operators competing with the former GM Buses fleet. Government insistence eventually forced the division of GMT into two companies, North and South. They must now compete with each other. And the passenger? Just as things were settling down so that he or she had some idea what colour bus to board and from where, Piccadilly bus station was closed for reconstruction and all trips between there and the Arndale Bus Station were banned to reduce pollution. Progress always has a price tag attached to it but it will be good to see the city back to normal.

Perhaps one saving grace for Manchester's bus operators is the sure and certain knowledge that the switch to rail, which took place after deregulation, is unlikely to occur again when Rail Privatisation occurs. In a perverse way the Conservative Government might yet make amends for the destruction of our integrated transport network when a healthy return to bus and tram travel becomes the most likely result of the forthcoming meddling with the railways. If through-ticketing becomes difficult, and a reliable timetable covering all services is already a thing of the past, what hope is there for rail travellers under a Conservative government?

The final section of this book shows the brighter face of the results of Deregulation, with a wide variety of liveries and makes of buses photographed in the glorious sunshine of 1995's heatwave. I suspect, however, that the scene is very different for regular – or worse, occasional – passengers catching the something past five on a wet night from an open bus shelter when they might not even know which is their bus out of the approaching procession.

Small wonder, perhaps, that the PTE's figures show more bus miles operated and less passengers carried, whilst the air we breathe declines in quality alarmingly.

The photographs show a selection of vehicles from the companies operating into the city centre. Such is the pace of change that almost from week to week there are different vehicles in different liveries and just as it seems safe to say that only three operators run Leyland Nationals another two introduce them! The spread of illustrations covers the former PTE companies, GMBuses North and South, the new giants Stagecoach, First Bus and British Bus, through the smaller operators down to those with just a handful of vehicles, together with brief details of the companies themselves.

It remains to be seen what the future months will bring in Manchester but if they are half as interesting as the last few months events have been it will indeed be another fascinating time.

Chorlton Street, arrival and departure point for express services.

Bee Line's City Shuttle picks up in Cannon Street, October 1995.

Bee Line has its origin in one of the early Deregulation companies set up for competitive service in Manchester. Manchester Minibuses Ltd was formed by United Transport Buses, a subsidiary of the British Electric Traction Group, in a bid to re-enter the British passenger transport industry. By the end of 1988, BET decided to pull out of bus operation and the Minibuses subsidiary (trading as Bee Line Buzz Co) was acquired by Ribble Motor Services. Within a year, Ribble was taken over by Stagecoach, the largest passenger transport group, whereupon a deal was agreed with the second largest group, Drawlane, which resulted in the transfer of Bee Line to that group. Bee Line remains with that group, now named British Bus PLC. The operator's name was recently amended to Bee Line Bus Co Ltd.

As the proportion of minibuses in the fleet declined, double-deckers from Ribble and from various British Bus subsidiaries entered the fleet, including the vehicle shown, when Drawlane took over certain Crosville operations in 1989. A 1984-built Leyland Olympian, it carries 77-seat bodywork by Eastern Coach Works.

After joining Bee Line, number 658 was first operated in Crosville green and cream with red on yellow Bee Line fleet name vinyl panels. Several varieties of red and yellow livery were applied to the batch of Olympians from Crosville before the current style, illustrated here, appeared. It was photographed in Portland Street, passing Chorlton Street on route 40 to East Didsbury, one of many serving the Wilmslow Road corridor and Manchester University.

Bee Line's vehicles are garaged at Hulme Hall Road, Manchester, with administrative offices at North Western's headquarters in Aintree, Liverpool.

This Bee Line minibus is one of the 50 Northern Counties-bodied 22-seat Dodge S56s which formed part of the fleet of Manchester Minibuses Ltd when operations commenced at the beginning of 1987, shortly after Deregulation. The minibus fleet eventually reached a total of 225 but many of these were withdrawn as double-deckers from various sources, and a handful of full-sized single-deckers, joined the fleet. Most of these were transferred within the group and some Mercedes-Benz midibuses were purchased new.

After passing to the Drawlane Group (now British Bus), Bee Line was later placed under the control of North Western of Liverpool and its diagonal style livery was applied to Bee Line vehicles for a time.

Recent recruits to the fleet are the 50 Metrobus double-deckers hired from West Midlands Travel (see below) and six new Alexander-bodied Mercedes-Benz minibuses.

Number 4 waits at the Piccadilly terminus of route 6 to Sale, though no destination is shown. Bee Line's minibuses could also be seen operating the temporary City Shuttle, designed to take passengers between the Arndale Bus Station and the Piccadilly Bus Station whilst the latter was closed for reconstruction from 17th September 1995, after the company was successful in tendering for the service.

By September 1994 many Leyland Atlantean double-deckers in the Bee Line fleet were between 15 and 20 years old. In order to reduce the age profile of the fleet, it was decided to withdraw or transfer the Atlanteans and to hire for three years 50 MCW Metrobus double-deckers dating from 1979 to 1982 from West Midlands Travel. This also had the advantage of standardisation for engineering purposes.

Many of these Metrobuses were pressed into service immediately, still wearing WMT livery, some with full West Midlands Travel fleetname, some with Bee Line fleetname and some with no fleetname at all. The first repaints were in the distinctive style displayed here by No. 802. Associated companies in the group followed the same style: North Western Road Car Co in red and blue and Liverline of Liverpool in two shades of blue. However, it must have been decided that this livery was too complex and labour intensive to apply, as the simpler style displayed by No. 658 (opposite) was adopted.

In this view number 802 passes the offices of Greater Manchester PTE as it approaches Piccadilly Bus Station from Portland Street with blind already set for the return journey to Rushcroft via Oldham.

BLACKBURN BOROUGH TRANSPORT LTD

Blackburn Borough Transport Ltd is one of the only 21 remaining (in 1995) Passenger Transport Companies set up under the Transport Act 1985 which required corporation transport departments to be formed as limited companies subject to the Companies Act. As the name implies, BBT is the successor to Blackburn Corporation Transport with the Council as shareholder.

The Transport Act enabled former territorial operators to register routes outside their traditional areas and BBT route X1 is an example, working from Clitheroe to Manchester. In this view, No. 204, a 1991 Volvo B10M-55 with Blackburn-built East Lancashire Coachbuilders 51-seat dual-purpose body is turning from Chorlton Street into the coach station at the end of its run from Clitheroe. It is followed by a Scania double-decker No. 1461, FWH 461Y, of GMB South, one of a batch of two purchased for evaluation purposes by Greater Manchester Transport in 1983.

The Blackburn livery of green and cream dates back to tramway days, though the shades and proportions have varied frequently.

BLUE BUS AND COACH SERVICES LTD

The original Blue Bus Service was formed in 1991 by two former senior managers from Shearings, Roger Jarvis and Alan Turner. The venture is based in the former British Rail railway works at Horwich near Bolton, and commenced with ten second-hand buses, mainly Leyland Leopards. The first route was between Horwich and Bolton on a 15-minute frequency timetabled evenly between the then GM Buses timings. Expansion quickly took place across Lancashire in the shape of new routes to Bolton, Chorley, Wigan and Manchester.

A wider expansion came in 1994 when a new company was formed, Yorkshire Blue Bus Company Ltd., to operate services out of Huddersfield where a depot had been acquired. Three coaches are also operated, all branded for Alfa Travel to which the company is contracted for tour work.

The fleet numbered 51 in September 1995, mainly consisting of Leyland Leopards. Three Dennis Darts and a DAF/Van Hool coach were purchased new and there have been a number of rebodies by East Lancashire Coachbuilders.

Of the eight double-deckers, No. 85, KSU 851P is illustrated here in Manchester's Lever Street Bus Station. The 76-seat Alexander-bodied Leyland AN68A/1R Atlantean was new in 1975 to Strathclyde PTE and was acquired in 1992 from ABC Travel of Ainsdale, Southport. The panoramic windows once favoured in Glasgow are apparent in this view and the type is unique to this operator in Manchester.

BLUEBIRD

Bluebird Bus & Coach of North Manchester has been run by father and son team, Tom and Mike Dunstan, since 1988. Tom, after service with Ribble and the original North Western Road Car Co, became managing director of the South Area of Greater Manchester Buses Ltd, and Mike was Piccadilly bus station supervisor with Greater Manchester PTE. Thus they were well-placed for deregulated operation in the Manchester area.

Most vehicles are minibuses, and several full-size coaches make up the 33-strong fleet. Number 88, F288 FLG is pictured here in Corporation Street, waiting to turn into Cannon Street on route 148, New Moston Circular, running to North Manchester via Newton Heath. It is an Iveco Daily, 49-10, with Northern Counties 22-seat body. New in 1988, it was a Northern Counties demonstrator, being acquired in 1990. Behind it is M8 BLU, one of six Marshall-bodied Iveco 59-12s purchased new in 1995, and built to comply with DIPTAC specification.

R. BULLOCK AND CO (TRANSPORT) LTD

Bullocks, based in Cheadle, Cheshire, is one of the oldest established operators in the Greater Manchester area, now directed by the third generation of the family. All classes of bus and coach work are undertaken, including local services following Deregulation.

A varied fleet including minibuses is operated, with many ex-Greater Manchester Transport Daimler Fleetlines joining the fleet to commence the local services. Despite the variety of chassis types, many of the buses and coaches have been powered by Gardner engines, including a Leyland Tiger coach, as there is much enthusiasm for this power unit.

Recently, five double-deckers have been bought new, including this Leyland Olympian (one of the last to be built as a Leyland) with East Lancashire Coachbuilders 76-seat body. Bullocks is one of several Greater Manchester operators now investing in new full-sized buses, these vehicles making a welcome addition to the bus scene in the City of Manchester. In November 1995 this operator became the first in the city to operate true 'low floor' single-deckers, four Scania L113/Axcess-ultrafloor vehicles being placed in service under the PTE initiative whereby such vehicles qualify for a grant towards their cost.

Most new vehicles carry personalised registrations, including L20 BUL, photographed here outside Manchester's Central Library in St. Peter's Square. Another one of Manchester's many architectural gems, the Midland Hotel, is in the background.

Bullock's livery has always comprised mainly red and white, though proportions and shades have varied considerably, and other colours such as black, pink and maroon have been added from time to time.

JP EXECUTIVE TRAVEL (CITY NIPPY)

J P Executive Travel is the operation of Mr J P Walsh of Alkrington, Middleton. The fleet of mini and midibuses comprises mainly Mercedes-Benz vehicles with small numbers of Iveco and Renault-Dodge. Routes are between Middleton and Manchester, and around Middleton itself, with a tendered service between Uppermill and Ashton-under-Lyne.

This 1994 Mercedes-Benz 709D with Marshall DP27F body is working route 131 to Middleton Bus Station and is pictured in Piccadilly leading a convoy of GMB South double-deckers.

The National Westminster Bank building immediately above the 131 route number once housed the BBC's North Region studios. The tower of the former Rylands warehouse at the left of the picture has appeared on innumerable bus photographs. This building is now Debenham's store.

CITIBUS TOURS LTD

For many years only one independent operator ran into Manchester city centre and this was Mayne of Manchester. However, from 19th May 1986, in advance of Deregulation, Citibus Tours Ltd of Chadderton introduced route 62 from Blackley into the city centre using a Willowbrook-bodied Bedford, this being a considerable breakthrough at that time. Also in that year Citibus operated the Station Circular services 5 and 6.

Citibus was founded in 1979 by Roger Green, a former Oldham Corporation bus conductor, and local man Martin Wild. It operated from a depot in East Manchester, moving to larger premises in Chadderton in 1989.

Commencing with four minibuses which were used on Education Department contracts, the fleet numbered 41 when acquired by the Lynton Travel Group of Hertfordshire in 1993 with Messrs Green and Wild continuing to run the business.

The livery was originally blue with black relief, seemingly without any gloss, a distinctly uninspiring combination, and ex-Preston Leyland Panthers were among the more unusual vehicles to see service on the streets of Manchester from this operator.

By February 1995, the fleet had grown to 63 buses, when the Lynton Group sold the company to Greater Manchester Buses North with the founders again remaining as managers of the separate subsidiary. By this time the livery had developed into two shades of blue with some vehicles carrying yellow beading. After takeover, several Citibus vehicles were repainted into GMB North orange, black and white livery but the double-deckers so treated were soon withdrawn.

The current fleet consists of Mercedes-Benz and Iveco Daily midibuses, Leyland National single-deckers, and Leyland Atlantean double-deckers from the South Yorkshire Transport (now Mainline) fleet. One of these, AN68A/1R number 641, XWG 641T, with 74-seat Roe body, is shown opposite in Piccadilly on circular route 160 to Moston.

R & M COOPER, T/A DENNIS'S

This operator's fleet has gradually grown to around 25 and comprises mainly Mercedes-Benz midibuses bought new. Also included are a handful of Leyland Nationals and a single Optare Delta full size bus purchased new in 1991. Livery is an attractive red and silver which continued from the coaches which had been operated since 1968. Local service operation commenced on Deregulation day in 1986 and this side of the business has grown until now there are no full sized coaches in the fleet.

M730 MBU is one of eight Mercedes-Benz 709Ds with Plaxton Beaver 27-seat bodies which joined the fleet in 1994. All are suitable for tendered work, incorporating Greater Manchester PTE's specification. The bus was photographed in Piccadilly on route 216 between Hyde or Ashton-u-Lyne and Piccadilly Bus Station.

Finglands is one of Manchester's oldest operators, dating back to 1907. It was one of the many coaching firms which ran to London prior to the effects of the 1930 Road Traffic Act. That route passed to the North Western Road Car Co Ltd in 1936.

The company has been well-known as a high-class coach operator for many years, also offering extended tours and providing the team coaches for Manchester City and Manchester United Football Clubs.

For most of its history the company was associated with South Manchester Coachways Ltd. The companies were eventually merged and the new title became Finglands South Manchester Coachways Ltd. In the mid-1960s this company took over next door neighbour C Holt of Rusholme, thus increasing both the fleet and the size of the premises.

With the advent of Deregulation, Finglands introduced local services, primarily for students between Manchester University and UMIST and the halls of residence along Wilmslow Road and Oxford Road, the operator's premises being conveniently located on the route. The success of this venture into bus operation brought about the expansion of routes into South Manchester and Altrincham, and the purchase of many double-deckers. Most of these were ex-Greater Manchester Buses Fleetlines and Atlanteans acquired from various sources.

The family-owned Finglands concern was taken over in 1992 by the Hull-based East Yorkshire Motor Services Group, created from the former National Bus Company subsidiary. It was East Yorkshire's first move outside its traditional operating area of Humberside and North Yorkshire. The new company name became Finglands Coachways Ltd and both services and fleet have continued to expand.

In September 1995 Fingland was one of the first operators in the city to place an N-registrered vehicle in service and N740 VBA, a Volvo with bodywork by Alexander, is seen wating to depart on route 41 to Sale Station. On September 17th the Piccadilly Bus Station was closed for demolition prior to redevelopment and the familiar structure behind the bus disappeared.

On October 13th it was announced that Finglands had taken over the Stagecoach Manchester company, including operation of the route 192 to Hazel Grove from Newton Street, seen on page 70.

Not all Finglands vehicles are as new as the Volvo, of course, and examples of older buses in use include ex-GMT KBU 912P, seen facing page left, which was acquired from Ribble Motor Services 1993 and was photographed in Princess Street on a short-working of route 48 to West Didsbury. This normally terminates at Northenden. It is an AN68A/1R Leyland Atlantean with standard NCME bodywork. Other similar vehicles in Finglands fleet carry non-GMT registrations.

The first new double-decker to be purchased for the fleet was F242 MBA, No. 710, later renumbered 1710, the Volvo Citybus seen on this page, and photographed during the morning peak hour. Running under the Metrolink overhead it was about to cross Princess Street, en route to Piccadilly via Mosley Street at the end of the 41 route from Altrincham. Its Alexander dual-purpose body seats 78 passengers and was originally painted white with bands below the upper deck windows in Finglands colours of brown, orange and beige. It was later repainted as shown here with more brown and narrower bands above the lower deck windows.

The Town Hall Extension, and the more distant Midland Hotel both look particularly fine in the bright morning sun at the height of the 1995 heatwave.

GMB NORTH Ltd

Greater Manchester PTE fought long and hard to try to persuade the Government not to force the sale and division of its bus company, Greater Manchester Buses Ltd, believing that the long-term interests of passengers and employees alike would be better served by retaining the status quo. It was to no avail and both North and South companies went to employee buyouts, the sales being completed on 31st March 1994, the Government's final deadline.

GM Buses North Ltd moved its administration to Oldham and retained depots at Manchester (Queens Rd), Atherton, Bolton, Bury, Oldham and Wigan. It took over some 965 vehicles and quickly began to place orders for new buses, particularly for use on the Whitefield/Bury corridor from the city where it saw opportunities to compete with Metrolink which struggles to cope with peak hour demand. It was also keen to promote an up-market image with high quality vehicles as will be seen again later.

Number 1057 was thus one of the first ten new buses to be purchased by the newly privatised company in 1994. The first five of the batch were painted in a livery of primarily pale primrose, dedicated to route 136 from Whitefield to Manchester. The remainder received basically orange fleet livery and were employed on route 135 between Bury and Manchester. However, certain vehicles were soon repainted in bright yellow, as was No. 1057 shown here on route 136 passing Manchester Cathedral. A further stage was the application of bright red 'Quality Choice' labels to the yellow-liveried vehicles for new routes in the Oldham and Wigan areas.

The Northern Counties 'Paladin Countybus' 10-metre bodies seat 40 with provision for 18 standing passengers. Maintenance of these vehicles has been contracted to Yeates Bus & Coach.

Shortly after the employee buyout, Greater Manchester Buses North Ltd embarked on a refurbishment programme for some of its older double-deckers, notably the integral MCW Metrobuses. Lacking the resources of the one-time central works at Hyde Road for such work outside contractors were employed to repanel and repaint, and in some cases modifications were made to rear number plate and route number panels, front destination displays and front grilles. With several hundred vehicles carrying the former GMB livery, orange and white were clearly going to remain predominant in any colour scheme

Number 5126 was photographed at the junction of Mosley Street and Piccadilly, having been repainted in GMBN's new livery which cleverly changed the appearance quite subtly by featuring a light grey central band and white stripes below the lower deck windows and above the black or charcoal grey skirt. Fleet numbers, on the grey band, are smaller than formerly, in contrast to GMB South, where the fleet numbers are larger and positioned on the front dome.

The Metrobus has just set out on route 59 to Shaw, Wren's Nest, via Oldham. To the left is the Piccadilly Plaza complex, and Lewis's store is at the right. Three GMB South buses are also in the picture and No. 4593 illustrates the South company's fleet number style. Following the temporary closure of Piccadilly Bus Station for rebuilding purposes, terminal points were moved to various on-street locations around the city centre.

GMPTE was conscious of the need to improve the quality of ride and service offered to passengers, particularly when Deregulation meant that other operators would be competing for the same traffic. Northern Counties, still owned by the PTA at that stage, were brought into the discussions and the result was a batch of standard Olympians fitted out to 'Express' specification, including provision of coach-style, high-backed upholstered seats. The vehicles were in course of delivery at the time of Deregulation and this example was delivered to the PTE as an operator, passing almost immediately to GMB Ltd on 26th October 1986. It retains its original attractive salmon livery, including the 'GM Express' logo, with the addition of the North company's logo. Note also the 'Express' title at the top of the destination panel.

Number 3242 has left the Arndale Centre Bus Station, seen in the background, and is turning from Corporation Street into Cannon Street at the commencement of its journey to Blackrod at the north-west extremity of the Greater Manchester area, a journey which will take some 72 minutes.

In addition to the Express Olympians shown on the previous page GMPTE also purchased two batches of ten MCW Metrobus coach-seated double-deckers painted in the 'Express' livery of mainly salmon pink with orange, red, brown and white. A further batch of ten was delivered later in 1986 and into 1987 to Greater Manchester Buses Ltd.

These vehicles were unusual in that the MCW Metrobus was intended to be an integral vehicle but, in this case, Northern Counties built the bodies on the MCW underframes. Northern Counties also fitted its own high-backed upholstered seats. Once again the aim was to offer a higher image and a superior standard of comfort to passengers on longer and limited-stop routes in an effort to encourage increased ridership.

All 30 vehicles passed to Greater Manchester Buses North Ltd in December 1993, and No. 5309, D309 JVR, was photographed as it threaded its way through Manchester's Piccadilly making for Piccadilly Bus Station at the end of the long route 67 from Cadishead, at the western edge of the Greater Manchester area. This example, fresh out of the paint shops, carries an eye catching 1995 version of the 'Express' livery featuring black window surrounds with pale primrose as the main body colour. It has to be said that GMBN is introducing some very attractive liveries – hopefully it will be able to keep them spruce through the dirty winter days to help brighten the city streets.

GMB North Ltd responded to competition by the introduction of several new batches of buses in 1994-95. Among these was a batch of 20 full-size 'Superbuses', though very different from the Bristol model of that name which ran on the city's streets in the late 1920s. These top-of-the-range single-deckers represent serious investment and are part of a major new vehicle strategy, having been intended to replace double-deckers on the Bury to Manchester route, on which MTL Manchester competed with new Volvo B6 midibuses. However, at the end of June 1995, MTL Manchester pulled out of Manchester in an agreement with GMBN which saw the Oldham-based operator relinquish its Liverpool aspirations. The vehicles now appear on other routes, notably 59 to Shaw and 67 to Cadishead.

Low-emission Volvo THD103KF engines are fitted, with ZF gearboxes with integral retarders. The Wright bodies, built in Northern Ireland, feature air suspension, kneeling facility and tinted double glazing. The Alusuisse-construction bodies contain 50 high-backed, moquette-trimmed coach seats which, it is hoped, will encourage more motorists to travel into the city by bus.

Number 505 of this batch is approaching Piccadilly from the ever-busy Oldham Street on service 135, with its electronic indicator display set for the return journey to Bury via Cheetham Hill. The promotion of the vehicle's virtues is in line with the modern competetive world's thinking – 'if you've got it flaunt it' is clearly the name of the game. It should be noted, however, that despite the bold branding these vehicles are not true 'low-floor' buses. Low floor operation is scheduled to begin in Manchester in December 1995 and GMBN is one of several operators responding to an initiative by ordering suitable vehicles which qualify for a cash rebate from the PTE.

The vehicle shown above left was one of the last of a long line of Leyland Atlanteans delivered to Greater Manchester PTE and its predecessors, the last of all being No. 4765, carrying the number 8765 until the renumbering of 1992. The AN68-D variant represented the final version of the model which was produced for the home market from 1958 - 1984.

Number 4760 was the first Atlantean to be refurbished by GMB North, in 1995, during which it received the North Company livery and a new destination display. It is shown here returning to the city on route 81, White Moss Circular (Blackley). The location is Victoria Street, with Manchester Cathedral in the background. Note how GMBN has created an attractive and instantly recognisable identity by the use of a colour scheme which breaks up the large expanse of orange.

It is noteworthy that at regular intervals since its adoption by the PTE in 1969 the orange has been progressively darkened from the pale shade originally applied. Many shades can be seen on vehicles in the city but it is interesting that during 1995 GMBN has been heading towards an even warmer shade of orange on some recent deliveries or repaints – shall we one day see a return to a full-blooded red?

GMB South has elected to retain more of the original GMBL livery, though the deeper shade of orange already mentioned certainly makes the vehicles look smarter. The livery has evolved steadily, taking in more black around the upper-deck windows for example, and during 1995 large roof mounted fleet numbers have appeared. In a concerted effort to bring the fleet to one corporate standard a policy of painting the lower deck panels and applying the new logos has made a considerable improvement at comparatively low cost when resources, financial and manpower, must be stretched.

The finished results from the two fleets can be compared in these two photographs, taken within minutes of each other as will be apparent. It is not immediately obvious that the GMBS vehicle is a Dennis Dominator, carrying the standard NCME body developed for the Olympian and itself designed for the PTE as shown above left. The main points of visual difference between the Olympian-type body and the original for Atlanteans or Fleetlines are the wide pillar at the rear of the first bay of the upper-deck, to accomodate the longer front overhang, and the enclosed engine compartment. H139 GVM, No. 2039, was delivered in 1991, the Dominator model dating from 1977.

Among the first vehicles acquired by Stockport-based GMB South Ltd after its formation in December 1993 were 23 elderly Leyland National single-deckers which were refurbished at the former North Western Charles Street, Stockport, works. Acquired from Amberley of Pudsey, this one, dating from 1975 and having 48-seat bodywork, was numbered 258 and the original registration LPR 937P was changed to the dateless SJI 4559. Other Leyland Nationals came from Gatwick airport and required substantial modification to remove their centre doors, offside and nearside, a legacy of their airside use by passengers at the airport.

The bold livery adopted by GMB South is a development of that of Greater Manchester Buses Ltd, as mentioned overleaf, with the addition of the contrasting company logo in blue. With blinds set for route 43, Woodhouse Park (Wythenshawe) to Piccadilly, No. 258 was photographed outside Boulton House in Chorlton Street with the service van in attendance.

This bus, 1755, C755 CBA, is the fifth of the original batch of twenty specially-built midibuses for Greater Manchester PTE's Centreline service between Manchester's Victoria and Piccadilly rail stations. Built in 1985, the Dennis Domino chassis carries a specially designed Northern Counties 24-seat body. This combination was an attempt to produce a small bus able to negotiate narrow streets in the business area whilst being built to heavyweight standards which would give the 'big bus' advantages in vehicle life, reliability, maintenance and part-replacement over the alternative van-derived midibus.

Number 1760 of the batch was borrowed by London buses in 1986 and painted in London red for a 3 month trial on route C11 from Holloway garage.

It was said when these vehicles were new that they should last for twenty years and all but two accident victims survive after ten years. For many years they were the first buses seen by rail passengers leaving Piccadilly Rail Station as they waited at their pick-up point at the top of the station approach. The inter-station link was no longer needed with the introduction of the Metrolink light rail vehicles running from Piccadilly to Victoria en route to Bury, and the Dominos were put to other work – they are still providing yeoman service on what is now the Centreline 'Shopper' route 5, as shown here, and other routes in Manchester and Ashton under Lyne.

Here No. 1755 retains its GM Buses fleetname after the split into the North and South companies. It was photographed leaving York Street before turning left into Portland Street to gain access to Piccadilly Bus Station. Note the improvement in appearance by the reduction in white when compared with the Leyland National, above.

Employee-owned GMBS acquired its first 'new' buses in a leasing arrangement with the Stagecoach Group. Twenty Alexander-bodied Volvo B6s were leased for twelve months to enable the operator to try out the vehicles with an option to purchase at the end of the lease period. The 40-seaters are numbered 301 to 320, and No. 319 was originally allocated to Stagecoach's Ribble fleet. Sharp-eyed enthusiasts will detect the former Stagecoach logo just visible through the GMBS white paint on the rear of the vehicles, below the rear windscreen.

Once again illustrating the investment which many Greater Manchester operators are making in new vehicles, the Volvo leads one of Bullock's new Olympians into St. Peter's Square en route to Piccadilly Bus Station.

As another part of its Deregulation policy GMBL invested in minibuses, of various makes and with varying degrees of comfort or otherwise. Many were little more than panel van conversions, part of the so-called 'bread van revolution' but others were engineered more along the lines of small PSVs. The 23-seat integral Metrorider was introduced at the time of Deregulation and a sales success was achieved at a time when many operators decided that smaller buses were appropriate to the new regime. The model was designed and built by long-established bus body builder Metropolitan Cammell Weymann which had commenced building integral vehicles with Scania running units in the early 1970s, gradually phasing out its other products. Later, an all-British double-decker was offered with a choice of engines.

Unfortunately, by 1989, production had ground to a halt, and the various divisions of MCW were sold off by its holding company, the Laird Group PLC. Metrorider production was taken over by Optare, based in the former Roe body works in Leeds. Optare dealt with design faults which emerged with MCW models in service, re-engineered certain items, and provided technical support to existing owners. A new generation Metrorider was later launched by Optare and this model continues to provide good service.

Greater Manchester Buses Ltd purchased 80 MCW Metroriders in 1987, most of which passed to the South company when it was formed in December 1993 and of which number 1621 is shown here in its GMB South livery. The blue GMBS logo is prominent in this view of the Metrorider, seen waiting by one of the JC Decaux smart city centre shelters forming its terminus in Piccadilly, and about to depart on route 11 to Southern Cemetery.

The Passenger Transport Executive, when still an operator, purchased 190 of these MCW Metrobus integral double-deckers. Number 5022 was one of the earliest, arriving in 1980. Both companies received allocations of the vehicles at the division following the management buy outs, this one going to the South company. Little has been altered, apart from the addition of the blue GMBS logo and the fleet number on the front dome. As this book went to press number 5055, the first of the refurbished Metrobuses in the GMBS fleet, appeared on the streets, sporting a completely white rear, from top to bottom, including the window area, prior to application of an all-over rear advert.

The blind shows 'Not in Service' as No. 5022 leads a line of former GMB buses out of the bus station into Piccadilly, past Lewis's store whilst a Metrolink LRV, Altrincham bound, can be seen to the right of the bus. During the closure of the bus station for reconstruction from 17th September 1995 buses were unable to come through in this manner, coming instead from Mosley Street straight to Market Street corner. No vehicles could use the left hand side of the road as shown here; buses which normally came from Oldham Street to gain access to the bus station were instead obliged to make a full circuit of Piccadilly.

When the privatisation of both halves of Greater Manchester Buses Ltd was completed GMB's coaching subsidiary, Charterplan, being already based at the Charles Street, Stockport headquarters of the new company, went along with the GMB South company.

Number 5, a Plaxton C53F-bodied Volvo B10M, pictured here entering Piccadilly from Oldham Street, was purchased new in 1985, being registered C167 ANA. It received a 'dateless' registration, OJI 9455, in 1992.

Charterplan coaches are used on all types of operation including excursions, tours, private hire and occasionally being pressed into service on GMB South bus services. However, in April 1994, GMBS retaliated against Stagecoach competition by attacking Ribble's X43 commuter and shopping service between Burnley and Manchester with Charterplan coaches. This competition continued for over twelve months until April 1995 when Stagecoach Manchester reviewed its fares and services on the 192 service from Manchester to Hazel Grove, reducing the number of vehicles used, and GMBS withdrew its X43 service 'on business grounds'. These vehicles are being used at present on GMBS service No. 201 between Manchester and Derby.

One of the most strikingly effective all-over-advertising buses seen in the city during 1995 has to be this GMBS Olympian carrying eye-catching designs for its sponsor, John Smith's brewery. One of the most interesting aspects of the design is its application over the windows, giving the impression of being opaque from the outside whilst allowing passengers to see out.

In another interesting development of the use of space to give maximum impact Metrobus 5055, mentioned opposite, has had a full depth advertisement applied to the rear of the vehicle, running from the rain strip at roof level down to the bottom of the engine compartment. Both window areas have been completely obliterated, unlike the Olympian shown here, and a striking graphic for a soft drink applied. This treatment is certainly eye-catching and it remains to be seen whether the maintenance crews will be able to keep the paintwork unsullied.

Number 2008, the Olympian, was photographed whilst waiting to take up its duty outside Manchester's Victoria Rail Station, yet another of the city's architectural gems and one seen for the first time in its true splendour when buildings facing it were demolished. Buses, trains and trams interchange here in Manchester's only real example of what passengers are entitled to expect in an integrated public transport system and a situation which would be regarded as commonplace and essential in any European city. Sadly, of course, this is not the city's principal rail station, having been demoted in favour of Piccadilly Rail Station which offers nothing approaching this degree of interchange or ease of access for passengers coming by private car.

A MAYNE & SON LTD

Mayne's of Manchester can trace its history back to 1920 when it was founded as a goods carrier and soon followed the custom of the time by fitting passenger carrying demountable bodies to the goods chassis. A regular bus service with passenger vehicles was running between the City Centre and Audenshaw by 1926. Mayne's operated as a co-operative with other small operators for a time under the fleet name 'Pioneer'. All the other Manchester independents were gradually taken over by the major operators, but Mayne's survived a token take-over attempt by Manchester Corporation to become the only independent bus operator in the Greater Manchester Transport area until 1986 when the Metropolitan County was disbanded. Its base is on Ashton New Road.

Out of a fleet of roundly 60, about one third are coaches and the company operates successfully all the coaching aspects, including continental tours, and an extensive bus service.

Although many second-hand vehicles have been acquired over the years, new vehicles have been purchased also, recently in the form of Scania and Dennis double-deckers and Dennis Dart single-deckers. All the Leyland and Dennis coaches were purchased new as were the pair of Bova Futuras, which are the company's flagships. Most coaches carry 'dateless' registrations.

Number 13, F113 HNC, a 77-seat Northern Counties-bodied Scania delivered in 1989, shows off the company's striking yet simple livery as it leaves the Lever Street bus station on route 232 for Carrbrook, Mossley, via Tameside Hospital, Ashton-under-Lyne.

For many years the only independent bus operator in the Manchester Corporation and, later, Greater Manchester PTE area, Mayne's co-operated with the Corporation and its successors on services to Audenshaw. After Deregulation, vehicles moved into Tameside, Droylsden, Oldham and Glossop and co-operation became competition under the new regime. Tendered services took Mayne's vehicles into Salford, Swinton, Eccles and Whitefield.

The Dennis marque is well represented in the Mayne fleet with modern Darts, Dominators and Javelins, and, from an earlier generation, five Falcon single-deckers with distinctive Marshall 'Camair' bodies acquired from Chesterfield Transport in 1991. Dating from 1984, the five – unique in Manchester – joined a Wadham Stringer-bodied Falcon acquired earlier in the same year.

The Falcon H type is a low-floor, single-deck chassis powered by a horizontal Gardner engine mounted under the floor at the rear in the manner of the Bristol RE. Although announced at about the time that the RE ceased production, the Falcon never gained the same popularity.

In this photograph, No. 48 has just left Piccadilly Bus Station and is travelling along Portland Street on route 290 to Trafford Park. The unusual roof outline can just be seen whilst in the background, the modern Hotel Piccadilly contrasts with the Britannia Hotel, magnificently converted from one of Manchester's many Victorian warehouses.

This 1978 built ex-London Buses Leyland Fleetline leads a line of buses out of Oldham Street into Piccadilly. Like its fellows from the London fleet, it was converted by Mayne's to single door configuration. Although many hundreds of these vehicles have been purchased after sale from London Transport's huge fleet only Mayne's operate any of the type in Manchester, though Lancashire United had some in the 1980s.

Number 34 approaches Piccadilly Bus Station with its blind already changed to 'Littlemoss' (Droylsden) in readiness for the return journey.

The white building in the background was once C & A's store. It has subsequently been converted into Sacha's Hotel.

MTL (MANCHESTER) LTD

Merseyside Transport Ltd was the former bus operating company owned by Merseyside Passenger Transport Executive which was sold to its workforce for £1 in 1992. Since then MTL Trust Holdings Ltd has been set up to act as holding company for newly created companies and other operating companies which have been taken over. One of the new companies was MTL (Manchester) Ltd which commenced operations in Manchester in 1993, later building up the fleet to over 150 buses and acquiring a depot in Miles Platting.

Investment in new vehicles was impressive and GMB North was quick to order new vehicles of comparative specification with which to compete on the Whitefield/Bury corridor. The expansionist period of the early '90s saw both the companies formed from the former GMBL operating in the Merseyside area and MTL continued to expand its Manchester operation. Eventually agreement was made between the companies and MTL's Manchester operation closed down on 1st July 1995 after agreements with both Greater Manchester companies for the mutual withdrawal of services in Manchester and Merseyside.

At the outset, East Lancashire-bodied Leyland Atlanteans from the Merseyside fleet were employed on MTL's Manchester routes. The original livery was a simple red lower half and cream upper half. This was later charged to the livery of cream and burgundy when it was adopted for the main Merseyside fleet, with the addition of fleetname in red and blue. This livery is displayed by Atlantean 1752, LKF 752R, seen in an attractive corner of Albert Square leaving Cross Street to run through to Princess Street as it works route 106 to Wythenshawe, having circled the city centre from Piccadilly Bus Station. The pressed metal plate carrying the fleetnumber, a Merseyside PTE characteristic located above the destination display, gives an immediate clue as to the vehicle's original ownership.

The bulk of the MTL (Manchester) fleet comprised Leyland Nationals from many sources, although that illustrated here, No. 6006, SKF 6T, built in 1979 and carrying 49-seat bodywork, was transferred from the parent fleet. It demonstrates the single-deck version of the attractive MTL livery, together with the prominent fleetname.

Leyland Nationals from many fleets can be seen in the city, as would be expected, in various colours and in various conditions. Few of GMBL's are to be seen now but at least three other operators still use the model.

The MTL National has stopped in St. Peter's Square, outside the Central Library, with the Metrolink light rail platform just out of sight to the left. It has travelled along the Wilmslow Road 'Corridor', used by so many of the Greater Manchester operators, and will continue forward along Mosley Street (shared with Metrolink) to the terminus of route 43 in Piccadilly Bus Station.

As competition intensified between MTL and GMB, the Liverpool operator decided to expand on routes to the west of Manchester, in the area between the two cities, and in the St. Helens and Bolton areas. As part of this strategy, all MTL-operated services working from St Helens depot were branded 'Lancashire Travel'. The opportunity was taken to employ a batch of new vehicles on these competitive routes and the 1994 delivery of full-size Volvo B10Bs with Northern Ireland-built Wright 'Endurance' bodies containing superior dual-purpose seating were lettered accordingly. The new MTL livery of cream and burgundy was applied, together with the brand name in standard style. These MTL services ceased on 1st July 1995 as MTL Manchester closed down.

Number 6508, L508 TKA, was photographed during the last week of operation, on route 68 leaving Manchester for Bolton, though no destination is shown. It is turning from Corporation Street into Cannon Street with the Arndale Centre in the background. This development incorporates a bridge over the upper part of Cannon Street.

METROLINK

Without doubt the most striking change on Manchester's streets is the reappearance of the tram, or more correctly, light rail vehicle. In a bold move to prove that investment in light rail will encourage people to forsake their cars and travel into the city using public transport the government, after much prognostication and considerable procrastination, finally gave the go-ahead for this system to be constructed. Owned by the PTE it was required to be financed with privately acquired money in an arangement where the system was to be designed, built, operated and maintained by the consortium which gained the contract.

The Italian-built articulated trams can be seen in the city, on street, between G-Mex and Victoria Station, travelling via Lower Mosley Street, Mosley Street, Market Street, High Street and Balloon Street, Shudehill. Certain sections of the route are shared with other transport, others are exclusively reserved for the use of the trams. At peak periods twin units operate. The system is proving successful in getting commuters out of their cars but since it is under-resourced in rolling stock its full potential has yet to be demonstrated. Twenty-six articulated sets operate between Altrincham, Piccadilly and Bury, using former railway alignments from Altrincham to G-Mex and Victoria to Bury. Extensions are planned and further competition with the area's bus network will take place when these eventually come on stream.

The system opened in sections from Spring 1992 and the workshops and adminstration centre are located at Queens Road, north Manchester. The Piccadilly Gardens station and trackwork replaces a portion of the former bus station.

The Central Reference Library provides the impressive backdrop for a BeeLine bus and Metrolink tram, both about to leave for Piccadilly via Mosley Street.

St Peter's Square with a north-bound Metrolink set leaving the station and a selection of buses making their way towards Piccadilly whilst in the right foreground a south-bound bus waits to cross into Lower Mosley Street.

Twin unit operation is impressive if restricted. Financial constraints in the initial phase resulted in there being insufficient power available to operate twin units at will. They are presently seen only in the morning and evening peaks with one double unit operating one trip in each direction.

MIDLAND RED (NORTH) Ltd

The 'Midland' name and distinctive traditional red livery of the once-renowned Midland Red company was revived in 1989 as demonstrated here by No. 1950, A150 UDM, a Leyland Olympian with Eastern Coach Works 77-seat body. It was photographed turning into the Albert Square section of Princess Street from Cross Street on route 129 to Macclesfield. New to the erstwhile Crosville Motor Services in 1983, No. 1950 passed to Midland Red (North) from the C-Line fleet when British Bus subsidiary company services in south Manchester were rationalised in 1993. As a result of this rationalisation the Macclesfield to Manchester routes passed to Midland Red (North) and thus the famous 'Birmingham' livery could be seen in Manchester.

In 1995 further rationalisation took Midland Red vehicles out of Macclesfield, to be replaced entirely by Stevensons, whose vehicles now run this service to Manchester as will be seen later.

The Leyland Olympian appeared at the 1980 NEC Show and after a chequered career continued in production under Volvo until 1993, thus having a life span of only about half that of the Atlantean. Its Leyland-designed body was built at Lowestoft, Leeds and later Workington whilst the underframe featured an all-steel perimeter frame, upswept at the rear to support the suspended engine, either Leyland TL11 or Gardner 6LXB. Other features were a dropped centre rear axle, air suspension and front-mounted radiator. Other operators using Olympians in Manchester are Stagecoach (Ribble), Bee Line and Bullock.

YORKSHIRE RIDER LTD

Yorkshire Rider commenced operation on Deregulation Day, 26th October 1986, as West Yorkshire PTE's arm's length bus company, formed as a requirement of the Transport Act, 1985. It became the first such company to be bought from its sole Passenger Transport Authority shareholder when it became the subject of a management-employee buyout in October 1988. It was one of the most successful ex-PTE companies and invested heavily in new vehicles. The Rider Group, into which it developed, was taken over by the Badgerline Group in April 1994. Badgerline merged with Aberdeen-based GRT Group to become First Bus PLC in June 1995, thus creating the second largest bus operating group after Stagecoach, pushing British Bus into third place.

Yorkshire Rider participates in National Express operations and consequently owns a number of coaches, mostly Volvo B10Ms and Leyland Tigers. Number 1421 is a 1991 Volvo B10M with Plaxton Paramount 53-seat body lettered 'Express Shuttle' for services between Leeds and Manchester and Bradford and Manchester. It was acquired from Park's of Hamilton in 1993. The location is Chorlton Street, the coach having turned from Portland Street and approaching the coach station. The elaborate architecture behind the coach, with its window canopies matching the coach's livery, belongs to the Britannia Hotel.

EXPRESS TRAVEL LTD

Express Travel evolved from Amberline Coaches of Speke, Liverpool, which had become part of the Drawlane Group, the predecessor of the major group, British Bus. Its former name is reflected in the personalised registration of this coach. Managing Director Ian Hann acquired the issued share capital from British Bus in 1994. After ten months of competition with National Express, Express Travel returned on National Express services while continuing to operate excursions, tours and private hire.

This photograph shows 1992 Volvo B10M-60/Plaxton Expressliner II K18 AMB, fitted with 46 seats and equipped with a toilet, on competitive service X80 from Newcastle to Liverpool, via Leeds and Manchester, about to enter Manchester's Coach Station. A notice in the nearside of the windscreen states that 'This is not a National Express Service'. Lettered 'The Extra Option', this highly-specified coach and its fellows represented an attempt to compete with National Express contractors on quality rather than price. Other routes carried dedicated liveries and were marketed as 'Executive Option' and 'Exclusive Option'.

The 25-strong fleet is made up mainly of Volvo B10Ms with Plaxton and Van Hool Alizée bodies, with three Van Hool-bodied DAF SB3000s.

NORTH WESTERN ROAD CAR Co LTD

The larger National Bus Company subsidiaries were split into smaller units prior to sale into the private sector. Ribble Motor Services was one such example, losing its northern operations to Cumberland Motor Services, and its Merseyside operations to a newly-formed company using the dormant company name North Western Road Car Co Ltd in 1986. This new company was sold to the Drawlane Transport Group PLC, now British Bus PLC in 1988.

North Western later took in the Crosville depots in Warrington and Runcorn, and moved its headquarters from Bootle to Aintree, Liverpool, though local services in the Manchester area were also operated. North Western took control of British Bus subsidiary Bee Line of Manchester in 1993 and services were rationalised, leading to interchange of vehicles for a time.

East Lancashire Coachbuilders Ltd of Blackburn became part of the Drawlane Group in 1988 and North Western ordered fourteen each of Dennis Dominator and Volvo Citybus double-deckers, bodied by East Lancs with high capacity 88-seat bodies of a distinctive design with a 'droop front' upper deck.

One of the underfloor-engined Volvo Citybuses is illustrated in the original (Drawlane) North Western livery of red, blue and white, applied diagonally. This was subsequently modified to a more easily applied horizontal version. Number 640, G640 CHF, turns into Albert Square on route 46 to Chorlton.

South Manchester Transport was set up in 1994 by three of the directors of Pennine Blue after that company was taken over by PMT of Stoke-on-Trent and Metropolitan-Cammell-Weymann-bodied Atlantean PHF 559T, built in 1978, was one of the first vehicles to join the fleet when operations commenced. It was new to Merseyside PTE in 1978, being withdrawn by its successor company MTL sixteen years later. The Merseyside batch carried bodies which were among the last to be built by MCW before the company decided to concentrate on the integral MCW Metrobus double-decker.

The South Manchester Atlantean is leaving St. Peter's Square for the run up Mosley Street to Piccadilly Bus Station, having arrived in the city on route 42 from East Didsbury. It leads GMB South Volvo B6/Alexander M742 PRS on route 50, East Didsbury to Piccadilly circular, with a Wall's Fleetline, ex-Greater Manchester, bringing up the rear. The South Manchester fleet includes double-deckers new to Merseyside and Greater Manchester PTEs, and single-deckers new to Rossendale.

ROSSENDALE TRANSPORT LIMITED

Rossendale Transport Ltd is one of the remaining 21 passenger transport companies still owned by its local authority. Bus operation dates back to 1907 when a Ryknield vehicle was purchased by Rawtenstall Corporation. Another arrived in the following year but the vehicles proved unsatisfactory and were withdrawn in 1910. Buses re-appeared in 1924 and from then onwards, Leyland became the standard make. Rossendale Joint Transport Committee was formed in 1968 when the Rawtenstall and Haslingden fleets were merged. The two former operators had shared a general manager for many years. Indeed, the general manager had three fleets to manage at one stage as Ramsbottom UDC was also under his jurisdiction. Deregulation in 1986 saw the limited company formed and to date, the Rossendale Council remains the sole shareholder.

Number 94, F94 XBV, is a Leyland Tiger with East Lancs 51-seat body, new in 1989. It is pictured here waiting at the layby in Corporation Street before proceeding to Piccadilly Bus Station on route 17 from Rochdale. Rossendale Transport acquired a depot in Rochdale after Deregulation and has developed services in the town and through to Manchester as seen here.

STAGECOACH HOLDINGS PLC

Stagecoach is Britain's biggest bus operator and continues to grow by the acquisition of other operators on a very frequent basis. It currently operates a fleet of some 6,000 vehicles, comfortably ahead of First Bus, the country's second largest. Its vehicles can be seen in various parts of Manchester, whether operating local or express services, and its commitment to purchase of new vehicles has been vital to the manufacturing sector which for several years after Deregulation was starved of orders for new buses.

Ribble Motor Services Ltd was one of the largest of the former National Bus Company subsidiaries and it was split into three parts prior to sale into the private sector. The central portion of the operations, based in its original home of Preston, remained as the reduced 'Ribble' company. This company was the subject of a management buyout in 1988 but in 1989 the management sold out to Stagecoach.

Stagecoach operates a corporate livery policy and Ribble's familiar red gave way to the group colours of white with orange, red and blue stripes, now familiar in many parts of the country. By 1993 the company name had become Ribble Buses Ltd.

A fleet of 23 Dennis Javelins arrived in 1993, fitted with Plaxton Premiére 47-seat dual-purpose bodies. Titled 'Interurban', these bodies were designed by Plaxton in conjunction with Stagecoach for use on limited stop services. One of Ribble's most popular limited stop routes is the X43 between Colne and Manchester via Burnley and the vehicle type was put to work on this service.

Competition was encountered with the Charterplan coaching division of Greater Manchester Buses South Ltd, operating older Plaxton Paramount vehicles, and a further seven 'Interurbans' were transferred from the Stagecoach South subsidiary in 1994. However, the competition ceased shortly afterwards.

Ribble No. 151, L151 BFV, is seen here passing Manchester Cathedral, about to turn into Cateaton Street en route to Chorlton Street Coach Station, approaching the end of its journey from Colne. In common with others dedicated to route X43, it is boldly lettered 'The Mancunian'.

Older vehicles in the Stagecoach (Ribble) fleet include this Leyland National 2 with Workington-built 44-seat bodywork. The National was built as the result of a partnership between Leyland and the National Bus Company but it was never as popular as had been predicted although its sound body construction and excellent anti-corrosion treatment ensured that the vehicles would be serviceable for many years. Many are now being completely refurbished and fitted with new engines but this example remains as built. Ribble operated a substantial number of Nationals and the survivors passed to Stagecoach on the sell out.

Number 815, YRN 815V, is an example of the Leyland National 2, introduced in 1980 with larger engine, the 680H of 11.1 litres, and front-mounted radiator which increased the vehicle's length by 0.3 metre to 10.6 metres in this case. Versions were also built to a length of 11.6 metres. It has received Stagecoach standard livery and is pictured in Corporation Street on route 27 bound for Bolton, via Swinton and Farnworth. The white building in the centre, standing at the foot of Withy Grove, was Kemsley House – later Maxwell House – once a famous newspaper headquarters in the days when many daily and evening papers were printed in the city.

Left: Stagecoach subsidiary Ribble used the fleetname Stagecoach Manchester for route 192 from Manchester to Hazel Grove, beyond Stockport. As part of its competition strategy with GM Buses South, new Volvo B6s with Aléxander 40-seat bodies were allocated to the service. It proved so successful that longer, 48-seat Volvo B10Ms were soon employed, all fitted with high-backed, upholstered seats for the high-quality operation. All the vehicles dedicated to this service carried a plan of the route on their sides. At the peak of the competitive operation GM Buses and Stagecoach between them were providing a 2.5 min headway at peak times. Following a reassessment by the two operators this was later reduced to more realistic levels.

Number 418, M418 RRN, a 1994 built example, was photographed in early October 1995 at the Manchester terminus in Newton Street with another of the same batch behind. It would pull forward for a few yards before turning left into Piccadilly and then proceed down London Road to commence its journey to Stockport and Hazel Grove. Shortly after the photograph was taken it was announced that with effect from 13th October the Stagecoach Manchester operation had been acquired by Finglands.

Facing Page

Stagecoach has invested considerably in new vehicles, and Ribble has received a share of this benefit. Volvo B6 and B10M chassis have entered the fleet, all bodied by Alexander and the quest for high quality services has required some vehicle transfers between operating companies. Aberdeen-registered No. 442, M799 PRS, a Volvo B10M with Alexander 48-seat body, was photographed in Corporation Street on route M10, to Brookhouse, via Pendleton and Eccles. One of Ribble's busiest routes, the M10 gained an immediate increase in ridership when the new vehicles replaced ageing Leyland Nationals.

Number 442 has just left the Arndale Bus Station on its service to Brookhouse, to the west of the city. Behind the Volvo is another of Manchester's architectural showpieces, the Corn and Produce Exchange, for many years the venue for the Manchester Model Railway Society's Christmas exhibition.

Lower left: Ribble received a batch of ten Leyland Olympians in 1985. The Eastern Coach Works bodies contained 67 coach type seats, and were painted in a special 'Timesaver' livery of white, grey and red for express services, especially those into Manchester from Colne and Preston. After the privatised company sold out to Stagecoach, the corporate livery was applied and three of the batch were transferred to Cumberland Motor Services of Whitehaven, another subsidiary company of the Stagecoach group.

One of the remaining seven, No. 2173, C173 ECK, operating with Stagecoach Ribble, is shown here on route X43 from Colne in Cannon Street, passing the Arndale Bus Station on its way to Chorlton Street Coach Station. The Leyland is powered by a Gardner 6LXB engine, an option which was available at the time the vehicle was built.

STEVENSONS OF UTTOXETER Ltd

Stevensons of Uttoxeter was formed in 1926 to operate in that area. It later took over East Staffordshire District Council, formerly Burton-on-Trent Corporation. Stevenson's 270 vehicles were acquired by British Bus PLC in 1994 and the company then became responsible for the Macclesfield services formerly operated by fellow subsidiary, Midland Red (North). As a result the Macclesfield to Manchester service is operated today by Stevensons.

Prior to 1972, Macclesfield depot was owned by the original North Western Road Car Company. When that company was split up the Macclesfield operations passed to Crosville Motor Services. Crosville was subsequently purchased by ATL Holdings and then by the Drawlane Group, now British Bus PLC.

Stevensons is well known for its wide range of interesting vehicles, and varying types can be seen in Manchester. The example shown here is a Leyland Lynx, normally an integral vehicle, but in this case bodied by Alexander (Belfast) Ltd. with the same style body as that standardised in the Timeline fleet, shown later. It is one of seven purchased from Belfast Citybus in 1992.

When so many coaches and buses are given Irish registrations to avoid the British year letter, it is interesting that HXI 3009 carries its original registration. Of further interest is that this Leyland chassis is powered by a Gardner 6LXB engine.

Number 259 was photographed in Mosley Street, waiting to cross the Metrolink tracks to gain access to Piccadilly Bus Station on route 130 from Macclesfield. The single carriageway becomes congested at this point as buses wait for the traffic signals to change, and interesting selections of vehicles can be seen waiting their turn, as here, reminiscent of days gone by when a wide and colourful variety of municipal and company buses would be seen in Manchester's Piccadilly.

STUARTS BUS AND COACH Co LTD

Scotsman Michael Stuart commenced Stuart's Coaches in 1979 with a single Bedford coach, originally under the company name Trimtrack Ltd. The business grew with more coaches, and local bus operation began with two routes between Haughton Green and Manchester shortly before Deregulation in 1986 in competition with Greater Manchester Transport. This competition continued when the PTE operation became a limited company, GM Buses Ltd., and today Stuarts continues to work along the Hyde Road corridor into Manchester.

One of the most interesting vehicles in its varied fleet is the 1992 Dutch-built DAF SB220 with Hungarian-built Ikarus 48-seat body, seen right, one of two which were dealer registered in Yorkshire by Hughes DAF of Cleckheaton. The decision to take into stock new DAF buses came after experience with a number of DAF coaches in the Stuarts fleet. Number 124 is seen leaving the city centre via Piccadilly and London Road on route 209.

Double-deckers include rare Marshall-bodied Leyland Atlanteans new to Sheffield Mainline, and two ex-West Midlands Travel double-deckers. Number 117 is an MCW-bodied Leyland Fleetline new in 1979, and acquired in 1990. It is seen leaving Piccadilly on its outward run whilst similar Park Royal-bodied Fleetline No. 116, WDA 680T, inward-bound from Haughton Green, carries this distictive black all-over advertising livery for Toyota cars. The

building behind the rear of the bus is the famous No. 55 Piccadilly, once the headquarters of Manchester Corporation Transport Department, now The Gardens hotel.

Fleet livery has always been mainly yellow and white but current bus colours are white with grey skirt and window surrounds with diagonal stripes of yellow, red and green. Many buses of Scottish origin have passed through the fleet. Coaches are of Leyland, DAF and Bova makes.

TIMELINE TRAVEL Ltd

Due to a change of policy when Shearings was taken over by the Rank Organisation in 1990, it was decided to withdraw from bus operation and to concentrate on the coaching business. The major part of the bus business was sold to Timeline Travel Ltd, a company headed by Ian Longworth, former managing director of Shearings Coach and Bus, in 1992. He had built up Shearings' bus business since Deregulation and at the time of the sale had achieved one of the most modern bus fleets in the north west. Most of the 66 buses were either Leyland Tigers with Alexander 'N' bodies or Volvo D10Ms with Alexander 'Q' bodies, all seating 55. The bodies were built in Alexander's Northern Ireland factory and few others are seen outside the Province. Shearings had established a distinctive vehicle design.

Most remain in the fleet, and while the double-deckers have been gradually withdrawn, the fleet has been updated with Mercedes-Benz midibuses, Volvo B6s and coaches, including seventeen new Neoplan Transliners. The former Shearings livery has been retained. Most of the 17 new Neoplan Transliners are in Highland Heritage livery, however, for Scottish tour operations. Interestingly this contract was won from Shearings.

Timeline operates from a depot at Lowton with its registered office in Leigh. It serves Bolton, Bury, Eccles, Manchester, Stockport and St. Helens, and there is a separate operation in Telford, Shropshire, retained from the Shearings operations commenced at Deregulation.

Number 67, G67 RND, is a Leyland Tiger with Alexander (Belfast) N-type body, photographed in Victoria Bridge Street crossing the River Irwell from Salford into Manchester. In corporation days, Salford buses lined up in the nearside lane at their 'Victoria' terminus.

The later batch of single-deckers which were new to the Shearings bus operation is represented by this Volvo Citibus D10M-50 with Alexander (Belfast) 'Q' type body seating 55. The modern fleet of single-deckers passed to Timeline when the bus business was purchased from Shearings in 1992. Similar bodies can be seen on vehicles operating into Manchester on Trent's Trans Peak service. Number 81, H81 DVM new in 1990, is shown here turning from Corporation Street into Cannon Street at the commencement of route X36 to Bolton.

At the end of 1994, the Timeline fleet had reached 110 vehicles, virtually all under seven years old. Investment continues with new Alexander-bodied Volvo B6s and Mercedes-Benz midibuses entering the fleet in 1995.

Yet another example of an independent operator investing in new vehicles, this Volvo B6 with Alexander Dash 38-seat body is one of six received in 1995. Six similar buses joined the fleet in 1994. Once again we see that new and high quality vehicles generate ridership. In this case, 31-seat minibuses are being replaced with 38-seat midibuses due to the growth in passenger numbers. Further orders were placed in 1995 for Mercedes-Benz minibuses with Alexander Sprint bodies. Because the full-sized Leyland Tigers and Volvo B10Ms taken over from Shearings' bus operation were purchased new, and the present policy is to purchase new midi and minibuses, this fleet has one of the lowest age profiles in the Manchester area.

Number 212, N212 WBA, is seen here leaving the Withy Grove exit from the Arndale Bus Station on route 137 to Bury.

The Arndale Bus Station is scheduled for major refurbishment, awaiting its turn when Piccadilly Bus Station has been completed. The low internal roof at the Arndale has prevented the installation of adequate extraction equipment, and the build-up of diesel fumes can become unpleasant and off-putting for passengers.

VALE'S COACHES (MANCHESTER) Ltd

Based in Cheetham, to the north of the city centre, Vale of Manchester also works on the famous 'Wilmslow Road Corridor', running into the city from the south. These routes cater largely for students at Manchester University as a common section links many of the halls of residence with the University campus. In this view, TPL 762X, a 1982 Leyland Tiger with Plaxton 53-seat bodywork, provides coach-style comfort on route 41 to Altrincham. A card in the windscreen announces that it serves Owens Park and Withington. After leaving the city centre, the route reaches Oxford Road and the main University buildings. Continuing into Wilmslow Road, it then passes Owens Park, the University's largest student residence, and Withington where there are many student 'bedsits'.

Vales commenced as a taxi business, a small coach company later being formed in 1988. This was subsequently bought out by what was known as the Ribble 'B'-team, the unsuccessful bidders for the Ribble company when it was privatised. The early bus operations consisted of tendered minibus services but the fleet now includes full-sized coaches and single-deck buses. At the time of going to press their service 335 operated the longest-unchanged timetable in the PTE area, remaining as it had been since 1988.

M J WALL

Michael Wall's fleet switched from coaching to bus operation at Deregulation and has gradually expanded to the present 45 vehicles. The depot moved from cramped premises in Fallowfield to a 2¼ acre site in Sharston, large enough to accommodate 100 vehicles. Wall's first service competed with GMB's route 42 from Piccadilly to Fallowfield along the Wilmslow Road corridor. Subsequent services were extended along Wilmslow Road to Didsbury, Northenden and Wythenshawe. A number of tendered and Sunday services are operated.

Bus operation began with twelve ex-GMT Daimler Fleetlines which were later joined by ex-GMT Fleetlines from other sources, Fleetlines from West Midlands Travel, Bristol VRTs and some short-lived Leyland Nationals. More modern vehicles have recently joined the fleet as shown on the following pages. Many of the Wall's older vehicles have received personalised registrations, some – as in the illustration – using the letters WAL.

The illustration shows 955 WAL, a 1975 Daimler Fleetline with Northern Counties 75-seat bodywork, one of the original acquisitions from GMT with which operator it was registered KBU 906P. It is leaving Piccadilly at the commencement of route 43 to Woodhouse Park, Wythenshawe with one of its fellows following. The selection of buildings behind the vehicles is interesting, showing that even in 1995 there is still considerable variety in central Manchester when it might be imagined that everywhere had been redeveloped.

Three of these Optare Star Riders joined the fleet in 1994 having previously served with Bebb of Llantwit Fardre. These views show the Optare front-end which replaces the usual Mercedes-Benz cowl, and the rear which displays Wall's globe logo. H83 PTG is the middle one of the three consecutively-registered midibuses used on circular services 46 and 47 between Chorlton, south of the city, and Victoria Rail Station, north of the city centre, once again serving the 'Wilmslow Road Corridor'.

In the background of these views is the fine facade of Manchester's Victoria Station, which caters for regional rail services and Manchester's Metrolink light rail system. The wrought iron work, incorporating the names of various destinations, both British and continental, linked up with a huge canopy which covered the roadway commencing approximately at the front of the bus. This was demolished in a spectacular accident in 1937 when a Sheffield bus struck one of the supporting pillars, causing the iron and glass structure to crash down on itself. Inside the station many features which recall its earlier life have been carefully retained whilst alongside the northern extremity the massive Nynex Arena development has recently been completed.

Several operators' vehicles use this terminus which is a stone's throw from many of the city's shops, the Cathedral and the world-famous Chetham's School of Music. Further re-development in the area is anticipated and Metrolink has done much to breathe new life into what was a very run-down part of the city across Corporation Street in the Balloon Street area.

Several Optare Delta single-deck buses, both new and second-hand, have been purchased by Wall's Coaches since 1989. G253 EHD, a 1989 example and one of a batch of three bought new, waits in York Street before moving into Piccadilly Bus Station. Route 101 runs into the city from Wythenshawe.

The Optare Delta was launched in 1988 and was described at the time as a futuristic design. The company had been created from the former Charles H Roe factory in Leeds and design and innovation were two of its first priorities. The visual appeal and positive design features of the Delta earned it the Bus of the Year award at the 1989 British Coach Rally, in Southampton.

The Delta body uses the Alusuisse method of construction for longevity, light weight and ease of repair. This Swiss-designed system consists of extruded and bolted aluminium frame sections, and panels which are easily removable from the outside. Front and rear are constructed in glass reinforced plastic incorporating easily replaced fittings such as separate corners, lighting units and bumper sections. The Optare body is based on the DAF SB220 underframe. Power is from a DAF 11.6 litre turbocharged diesel engine and transmission is by a ZF automatic gearbox.

It is encouraging to the promotion of bus services in Manchester that a number of smaller operators are investing in new vehicles now that Deregulation is well established. After putting into service a number of new Optare Delta full-sized single-deckers, as seen opposite, four new double-deckers joined the Wall's fleet at the beginning of 1995 in the shape of DAF DB250s with 77-seat bodies to Northern Counties' latest design, the Palatine II, and feature an ample luggage pen by the entrance. Voith automatic transmission, together with integral retarder was specified and the buses are fitted with kneeling front suspension.

The new buses were intended for use on Wall's W2 service between Gatley and Piccadilly Bus Station. M19 WAL was photographed on this service, setting passengers down outside Manchester Central Library in St. Peter's Square. It is followed by a comparatively rare Leyland Swift on Stevenson's service from Macclesfield. Both buses will move forward into Mosley Street, travelling along the northbound Metrolink tracks, before entering the bus station.

INDEX TO OPERATORS